Religious Education

and the Law:

A Handbook for Parish Catechetical Leaders

Mary Angela Shaughnessy, SCN

An initiative of the National Association of Parish Coordinators and Directors of Religious Education (NPCD) of the National Catholic Educational Association (NCEA), Department of Religious Education.

Cover and text design: Beatriz Ruiz
Editorial assistance: Cecelia Edwards
Publication assistance: Phyllis Kokus

Copies can be ordered from:
NCEA, Publications and Sales
1077 30th Street NW, Suite 100
Washington DC 20007-3852
202-337-6232
202-333-6706 (fax)
Special quantity discounts are also available.
See order form in back of book.

ISBN 1-55833-176-X
4th Printing, 1999

Dedication

This work is dedicated to the Sisters of Charity of Nazareth who have labored since 1812 to serve in the ministry of religious education.

Contents

Acknowledgements

T he NPCD Executive Committee and the NCEA Department of Religious Education express deep gratitude to Mary Angela Shaughnessy, SCN for providing such a helpful tool — one that is at once practical, succinct, and eminently readable. This volume along with its companion volume, *Religious Education and the Law: A Catechist Handbook* (published under separate cover), are a tribute to her dedication to making legal issues understandable to catechetical and educational leaders, and to her tireless devotion to placing these same legal issues into the context of ministerial care and concern for all who serve and are served in today's parishes.

Special thanks go to the readers who gave generously of their time and careful attention to critique the manuscript and who made valuable recommendations. These readers represent the active, dedicated involvement of both the NPCD Executive Committee and members of the religious education division of NCEA's Department of Chief Administrators of Catholic Education (CACE). Grateful acknowledgement goes to:

Anne Brown
NPCD Regional Representative for the Southwest
Holy Ghost Parish, Houston TX

Ginger Infantino
Director of Catechetical Ministry
Diocese of San Diego, San Diego CA

Maureen Kennedy, OP
Director of Religious Education
Archdiocese of Mobile, Mobile AL

Charlotte Sutherland
NPCD Regional Representative for the Northwest
St. Louise Parish, Belleview WA

Thanks also go to others essential to the successful completion of this project: Phyllis Kokus for attending tirelessly to publishing logistics, Cecelia Edwards for giving valuable editorial assistance and Beatriz Ruiz for her creativity in developing the cover and text design.

Preface

This year NPCD celebrates 20 years as the national professional membership association for parish catechetical leaders. The years from 1976 - 1996 have seen many successes in the work of the NPCD Executive Committee on behalf of the members. The regional representatives who make up this committee are parish catechetical leaders themselves, always attentive to issues emerging among their peers in parish ministry. This publication is an example of the effects of their listening to the needs and concerns expressed within their regions.

Soon after the NCEA publication of *A Primer on Law for DREs and Youth Ministers* by Mary Angela Shaughnessy, NPCD regional representatives began to hear the request for "more" — that additional topics of concern to catechetical leaders be addressed, and that a catechist resource also be created to orient them to their role in preventive measures that can be taken to protect all involved in catechetical programs. Practical resources were called for to help catechetical leaders and catechists better understand the legal issues facing today's ministers who are concerned for those in their care as well as their own reputations as ministers who abide by the highest ethical standards.

In response to these requests for assistance in understanding legal issues, this helpful volume emerged. Designed to be used in a variety of settings, it addresses various legal issues as they impact catechetical leaders in their administrative roles. Its companion volume, *Religious Education and the Law: A Catechist Handbook* (published under seperate cover) addresses the same legal issues in summary form, highlighting the catechist's responsibilities. That volume is designed as a handy reference to be given to catechists, substitutes, aides, board members, etc. for their reference during the year. It orients them to the importance and relevance of these legal issues in their ministry and can be used as a basis for inservice sessions (see Part 4 of this Handbook).

Throughout both volumes, the term "catechist" is used in the classic sense to designate one responsible for working directly with adults, children and youth in the ministry of helping them toward a greater understanding of their faith. For purposes of simplicity, the term "catechetical leader" is used as an inclusive term meant to designate the person accountable for the direction, coordination and/or administration of the diverse responsibilities within a parish offering catechetical, educational and formational programs. In the application of the information covered and its relevance to diverse parish ministries, the term "catechetical leader" can also be read to apply to youth ministers, deacons, those in formation ministries and others in parish leadership roles whose titles are too diverse to enumerate.

Both handbooks are designed as helpful resources. They are offered in the spirit of St. Thomas More who once observed, "It is a question of love, not law." May they be useful tools for you in your role as a minister of God's love — protecting and ensuring the safety of all whom you serve in Jesus' name.

Barbara F. Campbell, D.Min.
Associate Executive Director
NCEA, Department of Religious Education

Introduction

Today more than ever before lay persons are being asked to share in the catechetical ministry of the Church by serving as catechetical leaders, catechists, and religious education board members.

This handbook is designed to provide catechetical leaders and others involved in parish religious education with essential information concerning civil law and its impact on Church institutions and programs. It is not intended as specific legal advice. If legal advice is needed, the services of a competent attorney licensed in your state should be sought.

The information in this volume is arranged in four parts. Each section offers basic legal background to enhance the framework of your ministerial perspective. Issues are grouped according to how they might be addressed when helping catechists understand their essential role in ensuring the safety of all in their care. Part 1 covers issues related to catechists' professionalism in their privileged role as partners in handing on the faith. Part 2 is concerned with issues relating to their direct contact with students. Part 3 addresses some of the basic administrative issues that impact you directly as catechetical leader. Part 4 offers practical suggestions for putting what you've learned into the hands of your catechists. It provides a guide for your use of the companion volume, *Religious Education and the Law: A Catechist Handbook,* in helping catechists understand the implications of the information, reflect on it and apply it to the specifics of your parish setting.

The companion volume, *Religious Education and the Law: A Catechist Handbook*, treats the same legal issues in an abbreviated form. In that handbook the role and responsibilities of catechists in relationship to the topics are highlighted. The only exception is in Part 3. Since the issues addressed in this section are primarily issues relating to the professional role of the catechetical leader, only the first two topics of Part 3 are addressed in the *Catechist Handbook*, "Catechist and Family Handbooks" and "Boards of Religious Education".

It is my hope that these resources will serve as effective tools as you strive to bring love "in deed" alive in your parish setting. May God bless you and your ministry abundantly.

Mary Angela Shaughnessy, SCN
March, 1996

Part 1:
Legal Issues and the Professionalism of Catechists

CHAPTER 1

Religious Education and the US Constitution

C onstitutional law is one of the major sources of civil law affecting education in the United States today and is the main source of the law for the public sector. In the majority of public educational cases, persons allege deprivation of constitutional rights.

Deprivation of Constitutional Rights

Religious educators are probably familiar with certain constitutional rights. The First Amendment guarantees freedom of speech, press, assembly, and religion; the Fourth Amendment protects against unlawful searches and seizures; the Fifth and Fourteenth Amendments guarantee due process.

Public school educators and students can, of course, claim constitutional rights because the public school is a government agency, and those who administer public schools are government agents.

The Constitution protects persons from arbitrary governmental

3

deprivation of their constitutional freedoms. Persons in Catholic educational programs, however, cannot claim these protections because such programs are in private institutions administered by private persons.

These restrictions may seem unfair, yet a similar price is paid by anyone who works in a private institution. If a person goes to work in a supermarket, the person will probably be required to wear a uniform. The employee will not be permitted to wear a button advertising a different supermarket chain.

The bottom line is that when one enters a private institution such as a parish, one voluntarily surrenders the protections of the Constitution. A catechist or student can always leave the program or parish, but so long as the person remains in the institution, constitutional protections are not available. Thus, a religious education program does not have to accept behaviors about which the public sector has no choice and is even required to protect.

What cannot lawfully be done in the public sector may be done in a religious education program. For example, the First Amendment to the U.S. Constitution protects persons "rights to free speech" therefore, administrators in public schools may not make rules prohibiting the expression of an unpopular viewpoint.

A landmark U.S. Supreme Court decision in 1969, *Tinker v. Des Moines Independent School District*, 393 U.S. 503, produced the now famous line, "Students and teachers don't shed their constitutional rights at the schoolhouse gate." Since no such constitutional protection exists in the private sector, catechetical leaders may restrict the speech of both students and catechists. Free speech issues in Catholic educational programs rarely reach courts; other constitutional issues often do.

Fairness and Due Process

The United States Supreme Court ruled in 1985 in *New Jersey v. T.L.O.*, 105 S.Ct. 733, that public school officials may use a "reasonableness", rather than a "probable cause", standard in conducting searches of young people. Religious education programs and Catholic schools are not bound by this case, however common sense and Gospel respect for students as persons should govern searches in any programs sponsored by the Catholic Church.

Public entities must be concerned with constitutional issues. Religious education programs, while not bound to grant constitutional freedoms *per se*, are bound to act in a manner characterized by fairness. Some legal experts talk about a "smell" test. If an action "smells" wrong when a person examines it, it may be suspect. For example, if a catechetical leader were to tell a student and her parents, "You are dismissed from the religious education program, and I am not giving you a reason", an objective observer would probably find that the action "smells" wrong. Persons do have rights, even if not grounded in the Constitution, to be treated fairly. Dismissing a student and refusing to give a reason do not seem to constitute fairness. In the end, the actions expected of religious education programs may appear much like constitutional protections. In no area is this more evident than in due process considerations.

The Fifth Amendment to the Constitution guarantees the federal government will not deprive someone of "life, liberty, or property without due process of law." The Fourteenth Amendment made the Fifth Amendment and many other amendments applicable to the states.

Persons entitled to constitutional due process have substantive due process rights, property interests (that which can be the subject of ownership, including jobs and education) and liberty interests (freedom, reputation). Substantive due process involves moral as well as legal ramifications: Is this action fair and reasonable? Substantive due process applies whenever property or liberty interests can be shown.

The Constitution also guarantees procedural due process, *how* a deprivation occurs. In the public sector, procedural due process includes: *notice*, a presentation of the allegations against the accused; *hearing*; an opportunity to respond *before an impartial tribunal*; opportunity to *confront* and *cross-examine accusers*; and the opportunity to *call witnesses in one's own behalf.* In serious disciplinary cases in the public sector, a person also has a right to have an attorney present.

Religious education programs, while not bound to provide the whole panoply of procedural due process protections that public schools *must* provide, are nonetheless expected to be fair. An Ohio court, ruling in a Catholic school discipline case, stated that courts could intervene in private sector disciplinary cases, if "the proceedings do not comport with fundamental fairness": (*Geraci v. St. Xavier High School*, 13 Ohio Op.3d 146 Ohio, 1978). Fundamental fairness in a Catholic educational program is akin to, but not synonymous with, constitutional due process.

Federal and State Statutes

Federal and state statutes and regulations, many of which have constitutional bases, comprise a second source of the law affecting Catholic catechetical and educational personnel. If a statute requires that all who operate an educational program within a given state follow certain directives, then all educational programs are bound. So long as what is required does not unfairly infringe upon the rights of the Catholic Church and can be shown to have some legitimate educational purpose, Catholic catechetical and educational programs can be compelled to comply.

The only situation in which a Catholic or another private institution can be required to grant federal constitutional protections occurs when state action can be found to be so pervasive within the institution or program that the institution can fairly be said to be acting as an agent of the state. The key factor in state action is the nexus or relationship between the state and the challenged activity. Although litigants have alleged state action in Catholic educational programs, no court of record has found state action present in teacher or student dismissal cases in private education.

Since religious education programs are not bound to grant constitutional protections unless significant state action is found, litigants alleging a denial of constitutional due process will have to prove the existence of significant state action within the institution before a court will grant relief. It is very important for catechetical leaders and catechists to keep these facts in mind.

It is not uncommon for parents, students, or catechists to claim that their constitutional rights have been violated in a religious education program when, in fact, no constitutional rights ever existed in the first place. These realities need to be clarified very early in the relationship between a parish religious education program and its staff, parents, and students. One way to prevent possible misunderstandings is to develop and disseminate comprehensive handbooks which outline the rights and responsibilities of all persons in parish religious education programs. (For a complete discussion of catechist and family handbooks, see Part 3, Chapter 1: Handbook Development.)

CHAPTER 2

Negligence and the Catechist: What is Legal Liability

N egligence is the most common of all lawsuits filed against educators. Even though negligence is the "fault" against which catechetical leaders and other parish administrators must guard, it is also one of the most difficult types of case about which to accurately predict the judicial outcome. What may be considered negligence in one court may not be considered negligence in another. It is much better, obviously, to avoid being accused of negligence in the first place than to take one's chances on the outcome of a lawsuit.

Since negligence is an unintentional act or omission which results in injury, a person charged with negligence is generally not going to face criminal charges. Persons who bring successful negligence suits are usually awarded money damages in an amount calculated to compensate for the actual injury suffered. It is possible, though rare, for a court to award punitive or exemplary damages if the court is shocked by the negligent behavior. In assessing whether a person's behavior is negligent, a court will use the "reasonable person" test: would a reasonable person (catechist) in the defendant's situation have acted in this manner? "Reasonable" is whatever the jury or other fact-finder decides it is.

Courts also rely on the principle, "The younger the child chronologically or mentally, the greater the standard of care." Ninth grade participants in religious education programs, for example, would not ordinarily require the same level of supervision that kindergarten students need.

Some people believe that children and older students can never be left unattended. Such a belief is mistaken. Courts recognize that emergencies can arise and that students might be left alone while the supervisor is taking care of the emergency. Judges expect, however, that supervisors will have told students at other points, such as the beginning of the term and periodically thereafter, what they are supposed to do if the supervisor has to leave. At minimum, rules might require that students remain in their seats when no adult is present. Catechetical leaders should consider developing a catechist rule that students are not to be left unattended unless absolutely necessary, and that proper procedures are followed in the event of an emergency. Ordinarily, a catechist should be able to tell some other adult that he or she has to leave the students.

Religious education programs present many possible negligence situations. It must be frankly stated that the religious education program presents more legal risks than does the average classroom. Most often, students are not in the ordinary classroom setting, and it may well be more difficult to ensure that students understand and abide by rules and regulations. In some programs in which substitutes are used in the absence of the regular catechist, the supervising volunteer may not even know the students' names. He or she may not be skilled in teaching and classroom management techniques.

Catechetical leaders should insist that all persons who supervise students, even the individuals who are on the substitute list, participate in an orientation in which appropriate skills can be addressed.

There are four elements which must be present before legal negligence can be found:

- *duty*
- *violation of duty*
- *proximate cause*
- *injury*.

If any one of these elements is missing, legal negligence cannot be present.

The Element of *Duty*

The person charged with negligence must have had a *duty* in the situation. Educators are not responsible for injuries occurring at a place where or a time when they had no responsibility. A catechetical leader or a catechist, walking through a mall on a weekend, does not have a legal duty to students who are also walking through the mall. Within the religious education setting, students have a right to safety and catechetical leaders and catechists have a duty to protect the safety of all those entrusted to their care. Catechetical leaders have a duty to develop and implement rules and regulations guiding catechists in providing for student safety.

One situation that presents problems from a negligence standpoint is that of the student who arrives early and/or is not picked up at dismissal time. All catechists must understand that students must be supervised from the time they arrive at the religious education site until the time they depart. If parents are late picking up their children, an adult catechist or staff member must remain with the students until the parents arrive. Catechetical leaders may want to consider some sort of penalty for repeated violations of these rules. Perhaps a fine could be imposed, or a student could be denied participation in some social activity.

Whatever procedure an administrator chooses, at no time may a participant be left unattended or placed in front of a locked door to await the arrival of parents. Courts have indicated that administrators can be held responsible for participant behavior occurring on church property before or after programs and for the consequence of this behavior.

The 1967 New Jersey school case of *Titus v. Lindberg*, 228 A.2d 65 illustrates the extent to which educational officials can be held liable. In *Titus* the principal was found negligent and responsible for student injury occurring on school grounds before school because: he knew that students arrived on the grounds before the doors were opened; he was present on campus when they were; he had established no rules for student conduct outside the building, nor had he provided for student supervision. The court ruled that the principal had a reasonable duty to provide such supervision when he knew students were on the property before school.

It should be easy to see how a situation similar to that in *Titus* could arise in a religious education program. Who will supervise the early arrivals and the late pick-ups? This dilemma might well be taken to the religious education board for the development of a policy statement. Courts expect some policy as to when students may arrive at a program site, what rules they are to follow, and what kind of supervision will be provided.

In any situation, common sense has to prevail. Textbooks solutions are rarely available for persons working with young people. For example, a catechist who realizes on her way home that she has left an article at the religious education site and returns to retrieve it could discover that a student is outside waiting for a ride and no other adult is present on the premises. The reasonable catechist would wait with the child until parents arrive or until some other transportation arrangement can be developed. The catechist may think that it is not her responsibility because she normally wouldn't even be on the premises. However, a court could well decide that the point is that she was there and should behave in a professional manner. In the situation just described, a catechist may be tempted to put the child in her car and take him or her home. However, should a catechist elect to take such an action and an accident occurs, the catechist would be liable.

The Element of *Violation of Duty*

Negligence cannot exist if the second element, *violation of duty*, is not present. Courts understand that accidents and spontaneous actions can occur. If a catechist is properly supervising students during a break and one student picks up an object, throws it, and thus injures another student, the catechist is not responsible. However, if a catechist who is responsible for supervision were to allow object throwing to continue without attempting to stop it and a student were injured, the catechist would probably be found to have violated a duty.

Similarly, a catechist who leaves a classroom unattended to make a personal, non-emergency telephone call will usually be found to have violated a duty if a student is injured and it can be shown that the catechist's presence could have prevented the injury. If it can be shown that catechists often left students unattended while the catechetical leader, through inaction or inattention, did nothing about the situation, the catechetical leader has violated a duty as well. Under the legal doctrine of *respondeat superior* (let the superior answer), administrators are often held responsible for the actions of subordinates. In determining whether the superior is liable, courts pose questions such as these:

- Has the superior developed a clear policy for catechist conduct in dealing with situations such as the one which resulted in injury?
- Has the supervisor implemented the policy?
- Are catechists supervised?

The Element of *Proximate Cause*

The violation of duty must be the *proximate cause* of the injury. The court or jury has to decide whether proper supervision could have prevented the injury and, in so deciding, the court has to look at the facts of each individual case. Proximate cause is not necessarily synonymous with direct cause. For example, in the object-throwing example cited above, the student throwing an object would be the direct cause of the injury; however, the catechist's failure to intervene in the situation would be the proximate cause of the injury.

A well-known case which illustrates the concept of proximate cause is *Smith v. Archbishop of St. Louis*, 632 S.W.2d 516 (Mo. Ct. App. 1982). A second-grade teacher kept a lighted candle on her desk every morning during the month of May. She gave no special instructions to the students regarding the dangers of lighted candles. One day a child, wearing a crepe paper costume for a play, moved too close to the candle and the costume caught fire. The teacher had difficulty putting out the flames and the child sustained serious physical and resultant psychological injuries.

The trial court ruled that the teacher's act of keeping the lighted candle on her desk was the proximate cause of the child's injury. The court discussed the concept of *foreseeability*. It was not necessary that the teacher have foreseen the particular injury but only that a reasonable person should have foreseen that *some* injury was likely. The concept of foreseeability is important. Would a reasonable person foresee that there is a likelihood of injury? Religious education programs contain the potential for injuries like the one in *Smith*. Whenever possible, alternatives should be found to having open flames from candles. If lighted candles are used, extreme caution is in order.

Proximate cause is a complex legal concept. Religious education programs can pose special dangers when participants are not in the traditional school setting. Their energy can stimulate their taking risks that could expose them to dangers. Catechetical leaders would be wise to hold regular meetings to discuss the program, catechists' expectations, and foreseeable problems. These matters can then be analyzed in the light of health and safety requirements.

The Element of *Injury*

The fourth element necessary for a finding of negligence is *injury*. No matter how irresponsible the behavior of a catechist, there is no legal negligence if there is no injury. If a catechist leaves twenty first-graders unattended for thirty minutes and no one is injured, there is no negligence in a legal sense. In order to bring suit in a court of law, an individual has to have sustained an injury for which the court can award a remedy.

In developing and implementing policies for supervision, the catechetical leader must ask, "Is this what one would expect a reasonable person in a similar situation to do?" The best defense for an administrator in a negligence suit is a reasonable attempt to provide for the safety of all through appropriate rules and regulations. The best defense for a catechist is a reasonable effort to implement rules and regulations.

Because of the seriousness of the dangers posed by religious education programs, a greater standard of care will be expected of catechists than would probably be required of teachers in the traditional school setting. Catechetical leaders and catechists are expected to keep all equipment in working order and to render areas used by young people as hazard-free as possible.

Thus, catechetical leaders must take a proactive approach with regard to the elimination of hazards. All activities should be carefully monitored. All staff, paid and volunteer, should receive thorough and ongoing orientation and instruction. The reasonable catechetical leader supervises catechists. Practicing prevention by constantly striving to eliminate foreseeable risks will avoid costly lawsuits and injuries.

CHAPTER 3

To Copy or Not To Copy: That is the Question

Most religious educators realize that copyright law exists. If asked, many would probably respond that there are rules that should be followed when making copies of articles, book chapters, computer programs, and television broadcasts. Catechetical leaders and catechists have seen notices on copy machines warning persons making copies that they are subject to the provisions of the copyright law.

For some individuals, the fact that apprehension and prosecution for breaking the copyright law rarely becomes a reality seems to be a license to break the law. For others, their motive of helping young people is an excuse for failing to comply with the law.

One legal commentator has observed: "Although this act [copying] may appear innocent on the surface, copyright infringement, whether malicious or not, is a criminal act. One's position as a teacher and having 'only the best interests of your students at heart' does not give anyone the right to copy indiscriminately." (Merickel, *The Educator's Rights to Fair Use of Copyrighted Works*, 51 Ed.law Rep. 711, 1989).

Reasons to Copy

In the 1960s and 1970s budgetary considerations were the reasons given by churches, including Catholic Churches, that copied songs from copyrighted works and used the copies to compile parish hymnals. Courts have consistently struck down such uses and have ordered the offending churches to pay damages.

Today, church personnel appear to be aware of the legal consequences of copying and many subscribe to the licensing arrangements of music companies. For a given sum of money, the institution can make as many copies of music as desired during the span of the contract.

At the same time, it is not uncommon to find catechists copying such items as workbooks, other consumable materials, large portions of books and print materials. The swift advance of technology has catapulted computer programs, videocassettes and similar media into the sphere of widespread copying.

Copyright Law

Upon reflection, most educators would agree that copyright protection is a just law. Both the Copyright Act of 1909 (the Old Law) and the Copyright Act of 1976 (the New Law) represent attempts to safeguard the rights of authors. Persons who create materials are entitled to the fruits of their labors. Those who use author's creations without paying royalties, buying copies or seeking permission are guilty of stealing.

We may be tempted to think that copyright infringements and lawsuits are more or less the exclusive domain of large institutions. Certainly, we tend to hear about such abuses sooner than we learn of individual abuses.

Obviously, if a company is going to sue someone, it will seek a person or institution that has been guilty of multiple infringements so that larger damages can be won. It simply doesn't make good economic sense to sue someone who will be ordered to pay only a small amount of damages.

Sometimes, though, lawsuits are brought solely to prove a point. A relatively recent legal case, *Marcus v. Rowley*, 695 F.2d 1171 (1983), involved a dispute between two teachers in the same school. One teacher had prepared and copyrighted a 20-page booklet on cake decorating. The second teacher copied approximately half the pages and included them in her own materials. The amount of money involved was negligible, the author had sold fewer than 100 copies at a price of $2.00. Nonetheless, the court found the second teacher guilty of copyright violation; her use of the other's materials was not "fair."

What is fair use?

Section 107 of the 1976 Copyright Act deals with "fair use" and specifically states that the fair use of copies in teaching "is not an infringement of copyright."

The "sticking point" is what the term "fair use" means. The section lists four factors to be included in any determination of fair use:

- the purpose and character of the use, including whether such use is of a commercial nature or is for nonprofit educational purposes
- the nature of the copyrighted work
- the amount and substantiality of the portion used in relation to the copyrighted work as a whole
- the effect of the use upon the potential market for or value of the copyrighted work.

Purpose and character factor

Religious educators should have little or no trouble complying with the *purpose and character of the use* factor. Religious educators generally copy materials to aid the educational process. It should be noted, however, that recreational use of copied materials is generally not allowed under the statute.

Nature factor

The nature of the copyrighted work can prove a bit more problematic than *character and purpose*. Who determines what is the nature of the work—the creator and/or copyright holder, the catechist, the judge and/or the jury? Almost any material can be classified as educational in some context. Even a cartoon can be found to have some educational purpose if one is willing to look for it. It seems reasonable that, in determining *nature*, a court would look to the ordinary use of the work and to the author's intent in creating the work.

Amount and substantiality factor

The *amount and substantiality* of the work copied is especially troublesome in the use of videocassettes and computer programs. Educators understand that they are not supposed to copy a whole book, but may not understand that copying a television program or a movie onto videotape or copying a computer program for student use can violate the "amount and substantiality" factor.

In the case of *Encyclopedia Britannica v. Crooks*, 542 F.Supp. 1156 (W.D.N.Y. 1982), an educational company engaged in copying commercially available tapes and television programs for teachers, was found to be in violation of the Copyright Act. The company argued that it was providing an educational service for students and teachers who would otherwise be deprived of important educational opportunities. The court rejected the argument.

Religious educators may be tempted to think that their small-scale copying acts could not compare with the scope of activities in this case. In the majority of instances involving single copying, there is no comparison. A relatively new practice, developing libraries of copies, is emerging in some schools and religious education programs. Whether the collections are of print materials or non-print materials, such as videotapes and computer programs, the practice of building collections can easily be subjected to the same scrutiny as the *Encyclopedia* case.

Effect on the market factor

The last of the four factors, *effect on the market*, is also difficult to apply in the educational setting. Arguments can be advanced that students would not rent or purchase commercially available items, even if the copies weren't available. It appears, though, that use of an author's work without appropriate payment for the privilege is a form of economic harm. Good faith generally will not operate as an acceptable defense in educational copyright or infringement cases.

The court, in *Roy v. Columbia Broadcasting System*, 503 F.Supp. 1137 (S.D.N.Y. 1980), stated: "The federal copyright statute protects copyrighted works against mere copying, even when done in good faith and even when not done to obtain a competitive advantage over the owners of the copyright in the infringed works." (p. 1151)

Guidelines

A congressional committee developed *Guidelines for Classroom Copying in Not-for-Profit Educational Institutions*, printed in House Report 94-1476, 94th Congress 2d Sess. (1976). Catechetical leaders should ensure that catechists have access to copies of the guidelines, which are readily available from local libraries, the Copyright Office, and members of Congress. Although these guidelines do not have the force of law that the statute has, judges do use them in deciding cases. Some examples of the guidelines follow.

Meet the test of brevity

For poetry, copying of a complete poem of less than 250 words printed on no more than two pages or of an excerpt of 250 words from a longer poem is allowed. For prose, a complete work of less than 2,500 words or an excerpt from a longer work of not more than 1,000 words or 10% of the work is permissible. The guidelines mandate that copying meet this test of *brevity*.

Be spontaneous

The copying must be *spontaneous*. The catechist must have decided more or less on the spur of the moment to use an item. Spontaneity presumes that a catechist did not have time to secure permission for use from the copyright holder. A catechist who decides in September to use certain materials in December has ample time to seek permission. In such a situation, failure to seek permission means that the spontaneity requirement will not be met.

No cumulative effect

A last requirement is that the copying must not have a *cumulative effect*. Making copies of poems by one author would have a cumulative effect and would mean that collected works of the author would not be bought.

Similarly, the practice of *librarying* is not permitted. Videotapes may be kept for 45 days only. During the first 10 days, a catechist may use the tape once in a class (although there is a provision for one repetition for legitimate instructional review.) For the remaining 35 days catechists may use the tape for evaluative purposes only.

Conclusion

Catechetical leaders are responsible for supervision of all aspects of the educational process. If a catechist is charged with copyright violation, it is likely that the catechetical leader will be charged as well. Clear policies and careful monitoring of those policies can lessen exposure to liability. As many legal authorities have observed, copyright violation is stealing. It appears, then, that "Thou shalt not steal" remains a criteria for judging appropriateness.

CHAPTER 4

Child Abuse Laws and the Catechist

One of the most serious issues confronting educators today is child abuse. The media carry daily reports of adults causing children physical and emotional pain. The religious educator is in a particularly sensitive position. Children and adolescents often choose catechists as confidantes in their struggles to deal with abuse and its effects. For this reason, catechetical leaders must ensure that catechists and other staff members are as prepared as possible to deal with the realities of abuse and neglect. As the new program year begins, catechetical leaders would be well advised to spend some time reviewing pertinent state law, and diocesan policies and providing time for discussion of the topic at one of the first catechist meetings.

Statutory Considerations

All fifty states have laws requiring educators to report suspected abuse and/or neglect. While the actual wording varies from state to state, the statute will ordinarily be somewhat like that in Kentucky Revised Statute 199.335(2):

> Any physician, osteopathic physician, nurse, teacher, social worker. . . child caring personnel. . . who knows or has reasonable cause to believe that a child is an abused or neglected child, shall report or cause a report to be made in accordance with the provisions of this section. When any of the above persons is attending a child as part of his professional duties, he shall report or cause a report to be made.

Statutes generally mandate reporting procedures. The reporting individual usually makes a phone report which is followed by a written report within a specified time period, often 48 hours.

Statutes usually provide protections for a person who makes a good faith report of child abuse which later is discovered to be unfounded. Such a good-faith reporter will not be liable to the alleged abuser for defamation of character. However, a person can usually be held liable for making what is referred to as a "malicious report," one which has no basis in fact and which was made by a person who knows that no factual basis existed. Conversely, statutes usually mandate that a person who knew of child abuse or neglect and failed to report it can be fined and/or charged with a misdemeanor or felony.

Defining Abuse

What is child abuse? This author once heard an attorney define it as "corporal punishment gone too far." Although it excludes sexual abuse, the definition has merit. However, it poses questions: How far is too far? Who makes the final determination? Can what one person considers abuse be considered valid parental corporal punishment by another? Are there any allowances for differing cultural practices? It is difficult, if not impossible, to give a precise definition that will cover all eventualities. Certainly, some situations are so extreme that there can be little argument that abuse has occurred. A student who appears at school with cigarette burns has been abused by someone. When a child alleges sexual abuse, however, there probably exist only two conclusions:

- the child is telling the truth
- the child is lying.

The investigating agency will have to determine which conclusion is the true one.

The majority of cases will probably not be clear-cut and a catechetical leader may well struggle to decide if a report should be made. Many law enforcement officials and some attorneys instruct educators to report everything that a student tells them that could possibly constitute abuse or negligence. They further caution educators that it is not their job to determine if abuse has occurred. As a reporter, the administrator's or catechist's function is to present information. Appropriate officials will determine whether the report should be investigated further or simply "screened out" as a well-intentioned report that does not appear to be in the category of abuse.

In-service Education

Catechetical leaders should provide catechists and other staff members with some in-service training concerning the indicators of child abuse and neglect, and the legal procedures for reporting such conditions. There are many excellent written resources available. Local police departments and social service agencies are usually happy to make both materials and speakers available for in-service sessions. If a religious education program does not provide its catechists with education and materials on this topic, a phone call to appropriate sources should provide the catechist with needed materials.

Some of the most helpful material will identify warning signs or situations that should alert persons that abuse may be happening. For example, the National Center for Child Abuse and Neglect Specialized Training has identified the following six indicators of child neglect:

- lack of supervision
- lack of adequate clothing and good hygiene
- lack of medical or dental care
- lack of adequate education
- lack of adequate nutrition
- lack of adequate shelter.

The Center cautions persons to be sensitive to issues of poverty vs. neglect. Poverty is not synonymous with neglect. Poor children may need social services; they may or may not be neglected.

The National Center states that children who are abused physically or emotionally will display certain types of behavior which are survival responses to what is occurring in the home. Four categories of these behaviors include:

- overly compliant, passive, undemanding behaviors
- extremely aggressive, demanding, and rageful behaviors
- role-reversed "parental" behavior or extremely dependent behavior
- lags in development.

Who should file the report?

Many experts advise that the educational administrator, such as the catechetical leader, make all child abuse and/or neglect reports so that the same person is reporting all situations in a given educational setting. However, individual state laws may vary on this point. Every catechist and other staff member must understand that, if for some reason the administrator refuses to make the report, the catechist or staff member must file the report. If a catechist files a report, the catechetical leader must be notified that a report has been made. It is legally dangerous for the parish and program when a police officer or other official appears to investigate a report of child abuse, and the administrator does not know that a report has been filed.

Catechetical leaders, in conjunction with the pastor (and the parish school principal, if appropriate), should decide in advance how visits and requests from police or social workers will be handled. Many states require that educational personnel allow officials to examine and question students. Catechetical leaders should check with diocesan officials and seek legal counsel in determining the applicable law in a given state.

Educators and Abuse

A survey of recent educational cases decided in courts of record reveals that the number of lawsuits alleging teacher or other educational employee abuse of children is increasing. While administrators can be found responsible for the acts of subordinates, courts appear unwilling to hold administrators liable unless there is clear evidence of administrative misconduct. In the 1990 case, *Medline v. Bass*, 398 S.E.2d 460, educational officials were found innocent of misconduct in their supervision of an educator found guilty of abuse. The abuser's crime was outside the scope of employment and there existed no compelling reasons for his superiors to investigate his background more thoroughly than they did. In the 1990 case, *D.T. et al. v. Ind. School District No. 16 of Pawnee County*, 894 F.2d 1176, the court declined to hold school officials responsible for teacher abuse of students occurring during summer fund raising. A particularly troubling aspect of this case was the fact that the teacher had a previous conviction for sodomy. The decision notwithstanding, it is possible that, in situations in which an educational employee had a criminal record of child abuse, other courts may find administrators guilty of negligence if they failed to take reasonable steps to check references.

It is well established that schools and parishes can attract persons with abusive tendencies who are seeking young people upon whom to prey. Thus, it is important that catechetical leaders do everything in their power to investigate the background of persons before they begin work as catechists or other volunteers.

Some states now mandate that persons who work with children be fingerprinted; each applicant must also sign an authorization of a police check for any criminal convictions. Conviction of a crime is not an automatic bar to working with young people. Many states bar persons who have been convicted of a violent crime and/or sexual offense against children in the immediate past ten years. Administrators may wish to include a statement such as the following on applications: "Conviction of a crime is not an automatic bar to employment or to service. Please give all pertinent details. Decisions will be made as required by state law." For example, a forty year old woman who was convicted of stealing a car with a group of friends shortly after her eighteenth birthday, but who has led an exemplary life since, should not be barred from teaching religion.

Any student or parent complaint alleging abuse by a catechist or staff member must be thoroughly investigated. Failure to do so can put the parish and its officials at grave legal risk. Pastors, catechetical leaders, and boards of education should adopt policies governing reporting child abuse/neglect and investigating allegations of abuse by catechists *before* the need for such policies surfaces. It is preferable to have a policy that is never needed than to have no policy and be forced to try to construct one when faced with a need.

CHAPTER 5

Sexual Harrassment: What is it? What Does it Mean for Religious Education?

Today's catechetical leaders and catechists have probably heard much about sexual harassment. Newspapers carry stories of alleged sexual harassment and resultant law suits. No longer is sexual harassment something that is found only between two adults or between an adult and a child. School children claim that they have been harassed by peers. The news stories can seem overwhelming, and the potential for legal liability great. What, then, can catechetical leaders and catechists do?

They should first ensure that they understand what sexual harassment is. Every comment that is made concerning gender is *not* sexual harassment. For example, a male student who states, "Everyone knows boys are better at math than girls," or a catechist who declares, "I'd rather teach girls since they are not as rowdy as boys," is not guilty of sexual harassment. Title VII of the Civil Rights Act of 1964 mandated that the workplace be free of harassment based on sex. Title IX requires that educational programs receiving federal funding be free of sexual harassment. Both of these titled laws are anti-discrimination statutes.

Federal anti-discrimination law can bind Catholic institutions. Most parishes now file statements of compliance with discrimination laws with appropriate local, state and national authorities. Anti-discrimination legislation can impact parish programs because the government has a compelling interest in the equal treatment of all citizens. Compliance with statutory law can be required if a less burdensome way to meet the requirements of the law cannot be found.

The Equal Employment Opportunities Commission has issued guidelines which define sexual harassment, forbidden by Title VII as:

"Unwelcomed sexual advances, requests for sexual favors, and other verbal or physical conduct of a sexual nature when:
• Submission to such conduct by an individual is made explicitly or implicitly a term of employment;
• Submission to, or rejection of such conduct by an individual is used as the basis for an employment decision;
• And such conduct has the purpose or effect to interfere with an individual's work performance, or creates a hostile or intimidating environment."

The above definition concerns employment conditions; however, "education" can be substituted for "employment" in the definitions, and the basis for Title IX violations would be evident. Specifically, Title IX states:

No person in the United States shall, on the basis of sex, be excluded from participation in, be denied the benefits of, or be subjected to discrimination under any education program or activity receiving Federal financial assistance.

While the amount of financial assistance necessary to trigger protection has not been established, most Catholic parishes or parish-sponsored programs have taken some government funds or services at some time and, thus, would be well-advised to comply with Title IX as far as possible. Courts, including the Supreme Court, are vigorously supporting persons' rights to be free from sexual harassment.

In the case of *Franklin v. Gwinnett County Pub. Sch.*, 112 S. Ct. l028 (1992), the United States Supreme Court ruled that monetary damages can be awarded students whose rights under Title IX have been violated. In this case a teacher had allegedly sexually harassed a student for several years. The harassment consisted of conversations, kissing, telephone calls and forced sexual relations. The school system maintained that no relief could be given the student since Title IX remedies had been limited to back pay and employment relief. The court disagreed, held that students who suffer harassment are entitled to damages, and remanded the case to the lower court for a determination of damages.

Thus, it would appear that if Title IX applies to the Catholic school (and no case to date has held that it does not), students are protected against sexual harassment in much the same manner that employees are protected. Since religious education programs are sponsored by parishes in much the same manner as schools are sponsored, it seems that religious education program participants should also be protected from sexual harassment.

Actions That Can Constitute "Harassment"

The following are examples of behaviors that could constitute sexual harassment:

- sexual proposition
- off-color jokes
- inappropriate physical contact
- innuendoes
- sexual offers, looks, and gestures.

In a number of recent public school cases, female students alleged that male students made sexual statements to them and that school officials, after being informed, declined to take action and stated that "boys will be boys." The majority of these cases have been settled out of court and money has been paid to the alleged victims.

Although one can argue that the person who sexually harasses another should be liable and not the program and its administrators, case law is suggesting that supervisors who ignore such behavior or do not take it seriously can be held liable to the offended parties. (See *Jane Doe v. Special Sch. Dist. of St. Louis County,* 901 F.2d 642 (8th Cir. 1990.)

Suggested Policies

One of the most important actions a catechetical leader can take with regard to sexual harassment is to implement clear policies defining sexual harassment and detailing procedures for dealing with claims that sexual harassment has occurred.

The following is one suggestion of what should be included in a policy statement.

Definition: Sexual harassment is defined as:
- threatening to impose adverse employment, academic or disciplinary or other sanctions on a person, unless favors are given; and/or
- conduct, containing sexual matter or suggestions, which would be offensive to a reasonable person.

31

Sexual harassment includes, but is not limited to, the following behaviors:

- Verbal conduct such as epithets, derogatory jokes or comments, slurs or unwanted sexual advances, imitations, or comments
- Visual contact such as derogatory and/or sexually oriented posters, photography, cartoons, drawings, or gestures
- Physical contact such as assault, unwanted touching, blocking normal movements, or interfering with work, study, or play because of sex
- Threats and demands to submit to sexual requests as a condition of continued employment, grades or other benefits or to avoid some other loss and offers of benefits in return for sexual favors
- Retaliation for having reported or threatened to report sexual harassment.

Procedures for reporting

Procedures for reporting should then be given. These procedures should include a statement such as, "All allegations will be taken seriously and promptly investigated." Confidentiality should be stressed. Concern should be expressed for both the alleged victim and the alleged perpetrator.

Forms

Any forms that are to be used should be included in the explanation of the procedures for reporting.

Every catechist should be required to sign a statement that he or she has been given a copy of the policies relating to sexual harassment and other sexual misconduct, has read the material, and agrees to be bound by it. Parent/student handbooks should contain at least a general statement that sexual harassment is not condoned in a Christian atmosphere, and both parents and students should sign a statement that they agree to be governed by the handbook.

Prevention

It is far easier to prevent claims of sexual harassment than it is to defend them. To that end, employees, catechists, and volunteers should participate in some kind of in-service training that raises awareness of sexual harassment and other gender issues. All must understand what sorts of behaviors can be construed as sexual harassment.

Catechists should discuss issues of fair treatment of others with their students, and should promptly correct any students who demean others. Defenses such as, "I was only kidding," will not be accepted if the alleged victim states that the behavior was offensive and unwelcome and a court finds that a reasonable person could find the behavior offensive and unwelcome.

A recent incident will illustrate. During a religious education class, a boy and a girl approached the pencil sharpener. The boy stepped in front of the girl, sharpened his pencil, turned and blew the shavings on the girl's chest, and then swept his hand across the girl's sweater in the chest area as he stated, "Here, let me help you get that off." The girl and her parents complained. The boy was verbally reprimanded, but was not punished nor was he required to apologize. A lawsuit was threatened. It was determined that the parish had a policy, the catechetical leader was aware of it, but volunteer catechists had never been told of it. Although this case could very well have ended up in court, the parents declined to file the lawsuit.

Finally, of course, sexual harassment and other forms of demeaning behavior have no place in any religious education program. Guarding the dignity of all members of the parish community should be a priority for all catechetical leaders.

CHAPTER 6

AIDS, Blood-borne Pathogens and Other Diseases

The word AIDS evokes many emotions: fear, compassion, pity and anxiety, to name a few. Today's catechetical leaders and catechists are no strangers to these emotions. It is not surprising that catechists, like other educators have questions and concerns about AIDS and other blood-borne diseases.

AIDS and other blood-borne pathogens present discrimination issues. Lower courts have supported the right of students with such illnesses to education and the right of individuals with AIDS and other serious illnesses to employment so long as the disease does not interfere with their work and no one is placed in danger. The difficulty often comes, not with meeting those requirements, but with dealing with persons who discover that a student or employee has the disease. There are no easy solutions. A catechetical leader acting in accordance with the Gospel, cannot turn away individuals with these diseases any more than Jesus could turn away the lepers. Legally, a parish that would attempt to deny admission or employment to a person with AIDS or another disease may find itself defending a lawsuit alleging discrimination.

The catechetical leader who wishes to assess catechists' knowledge and attitudes regarding AIDS and other serious diseases may wish to use the following true and false pretest as a tool for beginning discussion and education. (Each statement is followed by a brief discussion.) For in-service purposes, a test sheet without answers and explanations should be prepared.

AIDS, the Law and the Religious Educator: A True or False Pretest

1. Students and catechists in programs sponsored by Catholic parishes have fewer rights than students and teachers in the public sector. (True)

   The rights of students and teachers in the private sector are governed by contract law, not constitutional law, since Catholic parishes and their programs are private institutions, not government agencies.

   Thus, students participating in a parish religious education program do not have the same freedom of speech and dress, for example, that public school students have. In essence, the United States Constitution, including the Bill of Rights, does not apply in the private sector.

2. Students and catechists in Catholic religious education programs are not protected by anti-discrimination law. (False)

   While the United States Constitution does not apply to Catholic programs, statutes and regulations do apply. Thus, a parish may not discriminate on the basis of race, sex, or national origin. Catholic programs may discriminate on the basis of religion. For example, a catechetical leader *could* determine that only baptized Catholics could enter the program. In actual practice, many religious education programs do not discriminate on the basis of religion.

The 1973 law, Section 504 of the Rehabilitation Act may apply to parishes. Section 504 requires that persons not be discriminated against *solely* on the basis of handicapping condition if they are otherwise qualified to meet the requirements of the position being sought. The Americans with Disabilities Act of 1992 provides further protection for persons facing discrimination because of disability. However, at this time, it is not clear exactly how the ADA applies to churches, and the case law is not yet developed on this point. Nonetheless, in the case of AIDS as a handicapping condition, the Gospel would compel us to do everything possible to meet the needs of the disabled, even if the law provides an exemption.

3. Catechists have a legal right to know if students in their classes are HIV positive. (False)

A number of court cases protect the rights of individuals to privacy. There would have to be some overwhelming, compelling reason to justify the violation of privacy rights.

One example sometimes offered is the situation in which a student is prone to biting. Legal experts suggest that clear evidence must indicate that there is a history of this kind of behavior, not merely a fear that such behavior might occur.

4. If two young people begin fighting, the catechist has a legal right to refuse to become involved if there is any reason to believe that he or she might be exposed to blood. (False)

The standard which determines the catechist's duty in any situation involving young people is the "reasonable person standard". The fact-finder in a court case must determine whether the catechist acted the way a reasonable person in the catechist's position would act.

A catechist has a higher responsibility to students than a stranger would have to them. There is a good possibility that a judge or jury would not accept "fear of coming in contact with blood" as a reason for a catechist to decline to protect students.

5. A parent has a legal right to know if a student in his or her child's class is HIV positive. (False)

Although parents may wish to know whether a child is HIV positive, current laws protect the rights of both parent and child to privacy.

6. A catechist may discuss a child's HIV status with someone who has an interest, other than mere curiosity, in the situation. (False)

A catechist, who may have been told of a child's HIV status by the parents or, with the parents' consent, by a parish official, has no right to discuss that status with anyone other than the parents or those authorized by the parents.

7. The catechetical leader always has a right to know if a student or catechist is HIV positive. (False)

The same right of privacy discussed in #3 and #5 applies to the catechetical leader as well.

8. If a student's parent or family member with whom he or she lives is HIV positive, the catechetical leader should be informed. (False)

While arguments can certainly be made that the catechetical leader should be informed in such situations so that appropriate support can be offered the student, there is no legal requirement that such information be given.

9. Universal precautions should always be used when dealing with any situation involving body fluids. (True)

Even if catechists and administrators know that certain students are HIV positive, there is no guarantee that other students are HIV negative. Persons who are HIV positive may not know that they are.

Currently, medical experts suggest that it can take two weeks to six months before one tests positive for the HIV virus, and up to 10 years before symptoms appear.

Thus, the prudent approach is to assume that everyone may be infected and to take universal precautions when dealing with body fluids. Every catechist and staff member should have gloves and disinfectant within easy access, and all program administrators should offer in-service training in this area.

Most dioceses have policies for dealing with blood-borne pathogens in schools and religious education programs. Catechetical leaders should be familiar with those policies and implement them in their own programs.

10. Since Catholic parishes and programs are private institutions, they may legally deny admission to individuals who are HIV positive so long as HIV status is not given as the reason for denial. (False)

Although there has not been a major case dealing with such a situation, it appears safe to say that courts would not uphold a denial of admission or employment in a Catholic institution to otherwise qualified individuals *solely* because of their HIV status. An individual denied admission or employment would have to offer evidence that would convince a court that the HIV status was the real reason for denial.

Nonetheless, an individual with AIDS could be denied employment or volunteer status on some other basis, if that other basis is job or status-related. A person who is too ill to perform the duties of a catechist can be denied a position as a catechist because he or she does not possess the *bona fide occupational qualifications* for the position, one of which would be the physical and mental capabilities of meeting the reasonable demands of the job.

The following recommendations might be the basis for ongoing consideration after the discussion of the pretest.

Recommendations

- Remember that everyone, including a person with AIDS, is protected against discrimination.
- Remember that everyone has privacy rights. Medical information is confidential and only those with a legal right to know can be informed.
- Assume that any catechist or student may be HIV positive or may have a communicable disease.
- Do not discuss the physical, psychological, mental or emotional condition of any student with anyone except parents and/or those the parents designate.
- Attitudes are important and can be expressed as much by actions as by words.
- Educators and other professionals are held to a higher standard than are "ordinary" people.

Conclusion

It should be clear that the law requires that institutions be nondiscriminatory. The fear of AIDS is real. It is the task of catechetical leaders and catechists to model Christian behavior and values. The question that should always be asked is: What would Jesus do if he were here?

Part 2:
Legal Issues and the Responsibilities of Catechists

CHAPTER 1

Students Rights and Administrator/Catechist Responsibilities: An Approach to Healthy Discipline

A
ll educational administrators face the challenge of respecting student rights while upholding discipline and order. Common law and common sense indicate that persons and institutions responsible for the education of youth are expected to hold students to standards of behavior. The main source of law governing the private institution is contract law. Nonetheless, the catechetical leader needs to understand the constitutional protections available in the public sector. Recent decisions have indicated that courts, utilizing contractual doctrines of fair play and arm's length

dealing, can require Catholic and other private institutions to provide protections that are very similar to those required in the public sector.

Due Process/Fairness

The Fifth Amendment to the Constitution requires that no person shall "be deprived of life, liberty, or property"... " without due process of law." There are two types of due process: substantive and procedural.

Substantive due process

Substantive due process can be defined as fundamental fairness involving moral as well as legal ramifications: Is this action fair and reasonable? Substantive due process applies when property (a right of ownership) or liberty (right to freedom or reputation) interests can be demonstrated.

Although not protected by the Constitution, Catholic students and parents have property rights in the contract between the parent and the parish. Courts can consider parent and or/student handbooks or similar documents as conferring property rights. Failure to protect the reputation of students can result in defamation liability in the Catholic parish in the same way such a failure can result in constitutional violation of liberty interests in the public sector. Religious educators should naturally be concerned with protecting the good name of all entrusted to their care. Disciplinary procedures, records, etc., may impact a student's reputation; care must be taken to guard against unnecessary harm.

Procedural due process

Procedural due process has been defined as a question: What process is due? In the public sector, several elements are present. In meeting the requirements of fairness, catechists should ask themselves these questions:

• What are our disciplinary procedures?

- Are they reasonable?
- Are all young people treated fairly and, as far as reasonably possible, in the same way?
- Is there a clear procedure that young persons and parents can expect will be followed?

Privacy and Access

Student privacy must be protected. Disciplinary and other non-academic records should be stored in files separate from permanent records. When a student completes the religious education program, only the permanent records should be retained in parish files. Parents have a right to inspect any and all records; all other persons should be denied access without written parental permission or a court order. (See Part 2, Chapter 2, Search and Seizure and Other Issues of Privacy, for further discussion of these issues)

A Historical Perspective

Prior to the 1960s, judgments were rarely made in favor of students. Courts instead invoked the doctrine of *in loco parentis* which holds that schools and other educational programs act in the place of parents, even if the educator makes decisions that parents would not reasonably make. The right of both public and private institutions to discipline was seen as absolute. This doctrine was largely abandoned in a series of cases beginning with *Tinker v. Des Moines Ind. School District*, 393 U.S. 503 (1969) in which the Supreme Court held that students in public elementary and secondary schools had First Amendment rights. Although *Tinker* has no direct bearing on Catholic religious education, it does reflect the willingness of the court to uphold student rights.

In a 1974 landmark case, *Goss v. Lopez*, 419 US. 565, the Supreme Court held that a student facing suspension should, at the very least, be given notice and some kind of hearing. The court's comments provide fruitful reflection for educators in both the public and private sectors: "[I]t would be a strange disciplinary system in an educational institution if no communication was sought by the disciplinarian in an effort to . . . inform him [the student] of his dereliction and to let him tell his side of the story in order to make sure that injustice is not done" (p. 580). One of the most significant Catholic school cases is *Geraci v. St. Xavier High School*, 13 Ohio Opinions 3d 146 (Ohio l978). In this case the state supreme court indicated that courts could intervene in private institution disciplinary cases if procedures were not fair.

Most education officials and attorneys would agree that the best education law is, like medicine, preventive. The best defense is having tried to follow the right course in the first place. Catechists and administrators must realize that, despite their best efforts in any and all areas of religious education, they may face lawsuits.

Courts look for evidence of good faith: Did the institution have a rule promulgated? Did the student know of the rule? The court does not concern itself with the wisdom of the rule-or even with the rightness or wrongness of the professional opinion of educators. The court is only concerned with the existence of a properly promulgated rule and with the institution's acting in good faith according to stated procedures. Courts look for basic fairness in the execution of the contract existing between the student/parent and the parish when the student is alleging that a parish official or catechist acted improperly.

Catechetical leaders must understand that it is impossible to identify everything a student might do that could result in suspension or expulsion. Therefore, it is advisable to have some kind of "catch-all" clause such as "other inappropriate conduct" or "conduct, whether inside or outside the parish, that is detrimental to the reputation of the parish". No court will expect an administrator to have listed all possible offenses, but courts will expect that *something* is written and that students and parents have a reasonable idea of the expectations of the program and/or parish.

Conclusion

The beginning point for rules development should be the parish or program philosophy. Harsh policies and procedures have no place in catechetical programs. Allowances must be made for the needs of young people. The guiding principle in any consideration of student rights and discipline should be the desire to act in a Christian manner characterized by fairness and compassion.

CHAPTER 2

Search and Seizure and Other Issues of Privacy

T he privacy rights of persons are treasured. One of the privileges of living in the United States is the right to be free of unreasonable governmental or other intrusion into the private affairs of persons. One main concern in this area is that presented by the issue of search and seizure.

The Fourth Amendment to the United States Constitution protects the right of persons to be secure in their persons and property. If a governmental agency searches persons and property without a warrant, the results of the search are considered poisoned and cannot be used against the person searched or the owner of the property. While it is commonly conceded that the Constitution does not apply in private settings such as those operated by churches, a review of the current case law involving young persons in public schools may be useful.

In 1985 the United States Supreme Court heard a public school search and seizure case for the first time. In *New Jersey v. T.L.O.*, 105 S.Ct. 733, a student was brought to the office of the vice-principal on suspicion of smoking. The student denied the charge, and the vice-principal began to search her purse. A package of cigarettes was found, and the vice-principal continued to search the purse which resulted in marijuana and other incriminating materials being found. The police were notified and charges were filed against the student who was later found guilty of possession of a controlled substance. The student alleged that her Fourth Amendment rights protecting her against unreasonable searches had been violated. The Supreme Court declined to find such a violation in this case. The court stopped short of declaring that students had no Fourth Amendment rights in the public sector. Rather, the court adopted a "reasonable cause", rather than the traditional "probable cause" standard used in public school searches. A public school official must have at least some reasonable rationale for conducting a search. "Fishing expeditions" to discover what contraband might be present, without more reason, are not allowed.

T.L.O. does not apply to private institutions, such as Catholic schools and religious education programs. Nonetheless, program administrators should have some kind of policy for searching students and/or seizing their possessions. Searching a student should require "more" cause than searching a desk or a locker.

Lockers and Desks

Lockers and desks are parish property. The catechetical leader and catechists have every right to examine them and their contents. A religious education program strengthens its position with students and parents by including a phrase such as, "The parish is co-tenant of lockers and desks and reserves the right to search them at any time without notice."

Search Situations

If a catechist believes that a young person is carrying a danger-ous item on his or her person, the catechist should ask the student for it. If the student refuses, the student can be asked to empty pockets, book bags, purses, back packs, etc. If the student still refuses, the catechist must make a choice. Obviously, if the catechist believes that persons are in danger, he or she will have to take whatever action appears necessary to gain possession of the item. If it is possible to contact the catechetical leader or another administrator, the catechist should do so before beginning a search.

If the situation permits, the best course of action would appear to be to contact the parent and have the parent come to the site and conduct a search of the student. Obviously, such a procedure is a serious one and should be undertaken only in appropriately serious circumstances. Where possible, catechetical leaders and other admin-istrators should contact the appropriate diocesan personnel or attor-ney for advice. The pastor should always be notified as well.

While constitutional protections do not apply, religious educa-tion programs and their personnel can be subject to tort suits of assault and battery and/or invasion of privacy if a student is harmed because of an unreasonable search. Carefully developed policies and proce-dures should guide any search and seizure; a common sense "balanc-ing test" should be applied in each case. Is this search and its possible effects worth finding whatever is the catechist or staff members are seeking?

For example, an exhaustive search for a student's lost dollar does not seem worth the effort. After asking if anyone has seen the dollar, the supervisor would be well advised to lend the student a dollar, if necessary, rather than to disrupt the educational environment by a search. If the young person has lost an expensive piece of jewelry, the catechist might conduct a more extensive search. Ap-proach is most important. Saying to a group of young persons, "Let's all help Johnny look for his watch. Let's all look in our book bags to see it could have fallen into one by mistake," while the adult supervisor examines his or her own bag, avoids the trauma of young persons being singled out for accusation. The dignity of each person and a commitment to treat everyone the way Jesus would should be guiding principles in any search and seizure situation.

Records and Privacy

An issue related to invasion of privacy is confidentiality of records. The content of student files should be released only to authorized persons. Even program personnel should be given access to files only for appropriate program-related reasons. Parental signatures should be required before records are sent to anyone.

Non-Custodial Parents

The issue of the non-custodial parent is a significant one today when so many students are not in the custody of both parents. Catechetical leaders may often find themselves facing a non-custodial parent who wants a copy of the student's records or other information. The Buckley Amendment grants non-custodial parents the right of access to student records. This Amendment binds public institutions. There is a difference of opinion among legal experts concerning the applicability of this Amendment to the private institution. Some scholars interpret the law as not affecting religious institutions. Others believe that religious institutions can be held to its requirements. There has been no case concerning the Buckley Amendment and a Catholic institution decided in any court of record. It is this writer's opinion that religious education programs, like Catholic schools, should voluntarily comply with the law. If one chooses not to comply, one runs the risk of becoming a test case in the courts. There are common sense reasons for allowing non-custodial parents involvement in the lives of their children. Unless there is a court order to the contrary, a non-custodial parent should be allowed to discuss a child's progress and should be given unofficial copies of reports, if requested.

Of course, a non-custodial parent has no right of physical access to a child unless granted by court order.

Religious education program administrators would be well advised to include a provision such as the following in parent/student handbooks:

> This program voluntarily complies with the provisions of the Buckley Amendment. Non-custodial parents will be given access to unofficial copies of student records, and catechists will be available to discuss the student's progress unless a court order providing otherwise is filed with the administrator.

An alternate inclusion would be the requirement that divorced parents file a court certified copy of the custody section of the divorce decree with the program office; such a procedure would help to protect the rights of everyone in the family.

Summary

While religious education programs are not held to the constitutional standards that public programs are, all catechetical leaders and catechists should be concerned with protecting the rights of young people entrusted to their care. Prayerful and thoughtful reflection and planning will help to ensure that programs have the necessary information, and that the privacy rights of persons are respected.

CHAPTER 3

Community Service Programs and Other Off-site Activities

P art of the mission of the Catholic parish is to teach service. The philosophies of most catechetical programs clearly state that one of the goals of the program is to develop persons who consider service to others a primary responsibility. To that end, many programs have initiated service requirements. These programs may range from preschool and kindergarten students visiting nursing homes at Christmas or adopting a nursing home resident as a grandparent to sophisticated programs at the high school level involving daily or weekly service at an off-campus site.

Many parents and students accept the service component of curricula. Some, however, question the necessity of, and even the right of the school to insist upon, service of all students. A few parents and students have been known to remark that, if you are forced to do the service, it isn't service at all, but some form of slavery.

Public schools have also initiated service programs and have received many of the same complaints that Catholic educational administrators have been fielding for years. A public school case, decided January 2, 1996 pinpoints some of the problems presented by community service programs. In *Immediato v. Rye Neck School District,* a second circuit New York case, 1996 WL 5547, a high school student and his parents brought a civil rights action against the district board of education. The Immediatos alleged that the district's mandatory community service program violated their constitution rights, particularly the Thirteenth Amendment's abolition of slavery, and the Fourteenth Amendment's due process clause. The district court granted summary judgment for the defendant school district, and the parents appealed to the U.S. Court of Appeals.

The district's curriculum included a mandatory community service program. All students are required to complete forty hours of community service at some point during their high school careers and participate in a classroom discussion about their service experiences. They must also complete a form documenting their service and de-scribing what they learned from the experience. Students are allowed to set their own service schedules and they must provide their own transportation. Student performance is graded on a Pass/Fail basis. No exceptions are made for students or parents who object to the service requirement. The program is governed by regulations concerning the types of organizations for which students may perform service, and the nature of the work that is undertaken. The students may not receive pay for their work. Twenty hours of the requirement may be satisfied by service to the school, but at least twenty hours must be completed at an off-campus site.

The court found that the community service program and in-voluntary servitude were not the same thing and that community service was not prohibited by the Thirteenth Amendment which abolished slavery:

In application, courts have consistently found that the involuntary servitude standard is not so rigorous as to prohibit all forms of labor that one person is compelled to perform for the benefit of another. The Thirteenth Amendment does not bar labor that an individual may, at least in some sense, choose not to perform....

On an interesting note, the court made reference to the 1925 landmark case, *Pierce v. the Society of Sisters*, 268 U.S. 510 in which the right of parents to choose private education for their children was upheld. The *Immediato* court noted that those who choose one school system for their children are free to do so. The Immediatos could have chosen a school that did not require a service program, even if it would have been inconvenient and/or costly to make such a choice. Thus, the court of appeals found that the public school's community service program was lawful.

In a 1995 North Carolina case, *Herndon v. Chapel Hill-Carrboro City Board of Education*, 899 F. Supp. 1443, a United States District Court reached the same conclusion as *Immediato* in a similar case.

Private institutions are not required to protect the constitutional rights of students, particularly any guaranteed by the First, Fourth, Fifth and Fourteenth Amendment. The question of Thirteenth Amendment involuntary servitude has not been addressed in the private educational setting. It is obvious that no institution, private or public, will be permitted to practice slavery. However, every action a student is required to take does not constitute involuntary servitude, even if the action is one the student would wish not to take. The findings of the *Immediato* case are important information for the catechetical leader. Since public schools, which are required to protect the constitutional rights of their students, may have mandatory service programs, Catholic educational programs certainly may have them. Administrators may wish to mention the *Immediato* case to questioning parents or students. Clearly, mandatory service programs are lawful.

Having established the legal basis for mandatory service programs, let us now look at some of the other legal issues which these programs present.

Parental Notification

The family handbook is a good place to provide initial notification of the existence of a mandatory student service program. Catechetical leaders should require that all parents sign a statement, "We have read and agree to be governed by this handbook," prior to their children's attending program sessions. It can then be presumed that the parents have read the handbook.

In the year or semester in which the program is held, the catechetical leader or program supervisor should notify the parents of participating students in writing of the requirement. The notification should reference the previously published statement in the handbook. Parents should be required to sign a permission slip authorizing student participation. The permission slip should state *where* the student is providing the service, and should state who is responsible for providing transportation. While some few parishes may transport students in parish vehicles, most parishes require that students or parents provide transportation. The permission slip should be signed by parents. A release from liability, prefaced with a statement that reasonable supervision will be provided, should be included. If a parent indicates a reluctance to sign, he or she should be reminded that the service program is part of the curriculum, and parental signatures are required for many aspects of student life.

Supervision

It is highly advisable that the supervisor of the service program visit all sites where students will be performing service. Such visits constitute appropriate diligence on the part of the parish.

Particularly if the service program involves released time from religious education, the supervisor should make spot checks of sites to ensure that students are in attendance and acting appropriately. If the sheer numbers and times of the service opportunities preclude such checks, the supervisor should be in regular phone contact with the site supervisor to ascertain that students are in attendance and that program objectives are being met.

Liability

The service program, like all off-campus programs, involves risks. One way to lessen parish liability is to ask each site to provide a letter of invitation to the parish religious education program. In this manner, any liability for injuries occurring on site should be largely borne by the site.

Other Activities

Community service programs are one type of off-site experiences. The issues addressed above should be addressed in any off-site activity. Service and other off-site experiences comprise an important part of the Catholic educational experience. Care and vigilance in the development and administration of such programs will enable all to reap the benefits of ministering to others in Jesus' name.

CHAPTER 4

Athletics and Other Types of Physical Activities

A thletics and other physical activities, including simple
play, pose legal concerns for all educational administrators. Catechetical leaders are no exception. With careful
planning and the development of clear policies and regulations, physical activity can be a rewarding experience within the religious education program.

Avoiding Negligence

Most lawsuits alleging negligence in educational settings occur
in the classroom or other instructional area, since that is where
students spend most of their time. Other areas however, are potentially more dangerous than the classroom. Hence, a greater standard
of care will be expected from catechists, staff and administrators.
Athletic programs are clearly activities that are more dangerous than

normal classroom activities.

Negligence is an unintentional act or omission which results in an injury. In deciding whether a supervising adult's behavior is negligent, a court will use the "reasonable person" test: would a reasonable person in the defendant's situation have acted in this manner? Would a reasonable catechist have left students unsupervised while they played basketball during a break? (See also Part 1, Chapter 2: Negligence and the Catechist.)

Before a court will find a person legally negligent, four elements must be present: *duty, violation of duty, proximate cause,* and *injury.* An examination of each of these four elements in the athletic/physical activity sphere should prove helpful to persons supervising such programs.

The Duty to Supervise

The individual charged with negligence must have a *duty* in the situation. Student athletes have a right to safety and supervisors have a responsibility to protect the well-being of all those entrusted to their care. Coaches are assumed to have a duty to provide reasonable supervision of their players. It is expected that administrators will have developed and promulgated rules and regulations which guide supervisors in providing for student safety. For example, if St. Monica's Religious Education program is sponsoring a softball team, the coach should develop and implement team practices that are consistent with safety and are in harmony with administrative practices.

Violation of Duty

Negligence cannot exist if the second element, *violation of duty,* is not present. Courts understand that accidents and spontaneous actions can occur. The 1989 New York case, *Benitez v. NYC Board of Education,* 543 N.Y.S. 2d 29, 541 N.E. 29, involved a high school football player who was injured during play. The player alleged negligence on the part of the coach and principal for allowing him to play in a fatigued condition.

A lower court awarded the student damages, but the appellate court ruled that school officials had to provide only reasonable, not extraordinary, care and reversed the decision. Further, the court invoked the doctrine of *assumption of the risk*. Students are under no compulsion to participate in organized sports; if they choose to participate, and their parents allow the participation, they voluntarily assume the risks of some injuries. *Assumption of the risk* is a defense against an allegation of negligence.

At first glance, it may appear that the coach or other supervising adult would be the persons found liable for violation of duty in the case of student injury. Under the doctrine of *respondeat superior*, let the superior answer, administrators, such as catechetical leaders, can be found liable for the acts of subordinates.

For example, if a catechetical leader paid little or no attention to the administration of an athletic program or organized play activity, provided no supervision, and/or offered no guidance, he or she might well be found guilty of negligence if a student were to be injured while a dangerous practice or policy was in place.

Unfortunately, many administrators believe themselves to be woefully ignorant of the principles of athletics and are too often content to let coaches and other volunteers run the athletic programs. These same administrators would be shocked if someone were to suggest that a catechist should be given a religious education text, told to instruct young people, and left to his or her own devices.

Administrators have an obligation to oversee any programs involving physical activities. While no one expects a catechetical leader to be an athletic or physical education expert, the catechetical leader should be sure that persons supervising such activities are competent to do so. The catechetical leader should insist that supervising adults keep the catechetical leader informed about the operation of these programs.

Students who participate in organized athletic programs should be given permission slips for their parents to sign. If any parents should refuse to sign the slips, their children should not be allowed to participate.

Administrators will not be held responsible for every mistake of adult supervisors, but only for those which a reasonable person could have foreseen. In the 1979 Virginia case, *Short v. Griffits*, 255 S.W. 2d 479, an athletic director was held liable for injuries sustained by a student who fell on broken glass while running laps. The school and the school board were exonerated. It was the athletic director's responsibility to ensure that the playing areas and equipment were in order. Unless the administrator had some reason to believe that the supervisor was careless in his oversight of the program, the administrator would not be expected to check the area for hazard.

Proximate Cause

The third requirement for legal negligence is *proximate cause,* which is a contributing factor. If a supervising adult were to organize a game in which thirteen year old students played against six year old students and the adult failed to establish and maintain safety measures, that inaction could be the proximate cause of an injury if a six year old were injured by an overzealous thirteen year old.

The court must decide whether proper performance of duty could have prevented the injury and, in so doing, the court has to look at the facts of each individual case. In an old, but still applicable case, *Stehn v. MacFadden Foundations*, 434 F.2d 811 (USCA 6th Cir., 1970), a private institution and its officials were held liable for damages sustained by a student who suffered a severe spinal cord injury in a wrestling match. The court found that the maneuver which resulted in the injury was not listed in any reputable book on the subject of teaching wrestling, and the defense could produce no evidence that the maneuver was legitimate. The court ruled that the school's violation of duty, its failure to ensure that the coach was qualified and experienced, was the proximate cause of the student's injury.

While it would be rare for a religious education program to sponsor a wrestling program, other intramural and intermural programs could be offered. It is imperative that the catechetical leader establish that supervising adults understand the rules of the game and are physically and mentally capable of providing the necessary supervision.

Injury

The fourth element necessary for a finding of negligence is *injury*. To prevail in a lawsuit, a person must have sustained an injury for which the court can award a remedy. Injuries do not have to be physical, they can be emotional or psychological as well.

Conclusion

Even if every possible precaution were taken, the possibility for student injury while participating in sports programs or other physical activity is very high. Administrators have very real duties to ensure that only competent persons are utilized as supervisors. Further, administrators must establish policies that provide:

- clear procedures to be followed when accidents occur
- minimal delay in seeking medical attention when needed
- hazard-free equipment and playing areas.

There is no absolute protection against lawsuits, particularly when physical activities are involved. Nonetheless, forewarned is forearmed. The catechetical leader who understands the risks involved in physical activity is better able to direct a religious education program that addresses the physical, as well as the religious needs of young people.

CHAPTER 5

Keeping the Confidences of Young People: What Can You Tell? What Must You Tell?

O ne of the more perplexing situations facing Catholic religious educators today is that presented by student sharing of confidential information. The young persons of the '90s may well face more pressures and problems than the young persons of any other decade. Broken homes, alcoholism and drug addiction, sexual and physical abuse, depression and violence were certainly found in earlier eras but they seem to be more prevalent, or at least more openly acknowledged, than they were when the majority of today's catechetical leaders and catechists were students. The responsibility for receiving student confidences and advising students in both day-to-day situations and crises can be overwhelming. Busy catechists and administrators may well ask, "What am I supposed to do? I know I'm not a professional counselor, a psychiatrist, or a social worker but I'm the one the student trusts, the one the student has consulted. Are there certain legal issues involved in the receiving of student confidences? Is there matter that must be made known to others, even when the student has asked for and received a promise of confidentiality from me?"

These are good questions for any catechist to ask. None of us can afford to think that we can help all students all the time. We cannot. If a student were to come to a catechist or catechetical leader and tell the adult that he or she is experiencing shortness of breath and chest pain, the adult would quickly summon both the student's parents and medical assistance. Yet, psychological problems are no less serious than physical ones, and the lay person who attempts to deal with such problems unaided may well be courting tragedy for both self and student. This chapter will address the following topics: confidentiality; legal immunity of adults, especially counselors; journal writing; and special situations such as retreats.

Confidentiality

Confidentiality is generally held to mean that one individual or individuals will keep private information that has been given to them, and will not reveal it. For example, the person who receives the sacrament of reconciliation rightfully expects that the subject matter of confession will be held sacred by the confessor and will not be revealed to anyone. Indeed, there are accounts of priests who died rather than break the seal of confession.

Friends share confidences with each other. One individual may say to another, "This is confidential. You cannot repeat it." The person speaking in confidence has a right to expect that the confidant to whom the information has been given will keep the matter confidential. But there are recognized limits to what friends will keep confidential. For example, if one's friend confides that she has been stockpiling sleeping medication and plans to take all of it that evening so as to commit suicide, it is not hard to see that morality demands that the confidant communicate that knowledge to a spouse or other family member of the confiding individual, or take some other action that would intervene in the attempted suicide.

It is not unheard of for an adult, who would not hesitate to get help for a friend, to believe that a student who is talking about suicide is not serious, can be talked out of the planned action, or is not capable of carrying out a threatened suicide. As child and adolescent psychologists report, young people do not usually comprehend the finality of death and do not think through the long-term ramifications of a suicide attempt. There is also, among some young people, a fascination with death as can be seen by the idolization of famous people who have died young or committed suicide.

If a student tells a catechist that he or she is going to harm self or others, the catechist must reveal that information even if a promise of confidentiality has been given. In a number of lawsuits brought against teachers and school districts, parents sought damages from teachers who were told by students in confidence that they planned to harm themselves or others. The teachers did not contact parents or other authorities. In some cases, the educators were held to be negligent in failing to warn.

Legal Immunity

It is a widely held myth that counselors, physicians, psychologists, and social workers have legal immunity from responsibility for any injuries that may arise from their not acting on confidential information presented to them. Most states have abolished counselor immunity, and the few who still "have it on the books" have imposed severe limitations on the concept. A counselor who hears from a young person that the individual plans to kill his or her parents and does nothing about it will not be legally able to decline to answer questions under oath nor will the counselor be held harmless for any resulting injuries if he or she decides not to reveal the threats. Counselors and other adults must make it very clear to confiding individuals that they will keep their confidences unless their own health, life or safety or those of another are involved.

The only two privileges from disclosure of confidential information which seem to remain in state law are that of priest/penitent and attorney/client. Even the husband/wife privilege which allowed a spouse to refuse to testify against a spouse has been largely abandoned.

In light of the above facts, a catechist must presume that no legal protection exists for those who receive student confidences. What should the adult do who wants to be a role model for young persons, who wants to be approachable and helpful? The answer is simple: lay down the ground rules for confidentiality before you receive any confidences. Tell students you will respect their confidences except in cases of life, health and safety. If a student asks to talk to you in confidence, reiterate the ground rules before the student begins to share.

Journal Writing

Religious educators have long recognized the value of student journal writing. This practice does, however, carry a real risk of student disclosure of information that the adult is compelled to reveal. Catechists must set the same rules for confidentiality as are discussed above.

Catechists must understand that they *are* expected to read what students write. If the catechist cannot read the assignment, then the assignment should not be made. Journal writing has a place in today's religious education curriculum, but adults must be sure that students understand the parameters of the assignment and of the adult's responsibilities of reporting threatened danger.

In one very relevant school case involving confidentiality, *Brooks v. Logan and Joint District No. 2,* 903 P.2d 73 (1995), parents of a student who had committed suicide filed an action for wrongful death and a claim for negligent infliction of emotional distress against a teacher who had assigned the keeping of journals to her class.

Jeff Brooks was a student at Meridian High School and was assigned to Ms. Logan's English class. Students were asked to make entries into a daily journal as part of their English composition work. For a period of four months prior to his death, Jeff wrote in his journal.

After his death, Ms. Logan read through the entries and gave the journal to a school counselor, who delivered it to Jeff's parents. Jeff had made journal entries which indicated that he was depressed and that he was contemplating suicide.

Ms. Logan maintained that Jeff had requested that she not read his entries, so that he would feel free to express himself. The journal contained a note in which Ms. Logan stated that she would not read the journal for content, but would only check for dates and length. The parents maintained that, in a conversation with Ms. Logan after their receipt of the journal, she stated that she had "reread the entries." Ms. Logan denied that she made that statement, and contends that she did not read the entries in question until after Jeff's death.

The lower court granted summary judgment in favor of the teacher and the school district. However, the appellate court reversed the finding, and held that there were issues of fact in existence which could only be determined at trial.

Thus, a trial court will have to determine whether Ms. Logan's actions or inactions constituted negligence contributing to Jeff's death. Part of the analysis will have to include a determination as to whether Jeff's suicide was foreseeable: would a reasonable person in Ms. Logan's place have recognized the possibility of suicide and notified someone. The appellate court refers to case law in which jailers have been held liable for the suicide of prisoners when the prisoners had exhibited warning signs.

Retreats and Other Faith Sharing Settings

The retreat experience is extremely important for today's Catholic young people. However, students are often at their most vulnerable in such situations. They may share stories of child abuse, sexual harassment, family dysfunction, even possible criminal activity. While encouraging students to share, the group leader must once again set the ground rules before the sharing begins. The use of peer leaders does not lessen the responsibility of the supervising adults. Student leaders must be told of the ground rules and of the necessity to communicate them to group members as well as procedures to be followed in notifying adults if matter is revealed in sessions that must be reported.

Conclusion

The Brooks case and the discussion in this chapter indicate the vulnerability of adults who receive student confidences. The wise catechetical leader will establish and enforce ground rules for dealing with student confidences, and will seek help from diocesan officials and/or parents when appropriate.

CHAPTER 6

Defamation of Character and Catechetical Programs

"Can I be sued for what I say about a young person?" is a question often asked by catechists who want to do the right thing for students but who want to protect themselves as well. The simple answer to the question is, "Yes, you can be sued." Catechetical leaders and catechists are wise to be concerned about what they say. Some basic information may prove helpful in establishing a philosophical and practical framework for statements made about the young people entrusted to one's care.

What is Defamation?

Defamation is a type of *tort*, a civil wrong. Persons who bring defamation suits will have their claims heard in civil, not criminal, courts. Persons who allege defamation seek money damages, not the criminal convictions of the person(s) who defamed them. Defamation of character involves twin *torts:* slander, which is spoken, and libel, which is written. Defamation is an unprivileged communication, i.e., a statement made by one person to a third party who is not privileged to receive it.

In any educational or ministerial setting, a court might well inquire as to the necessity for the communication. If the communication is found to be unnecessary, even if true, the court could find the individual charged to be, in fact, guilty of defamation.

Black's Law Dictionary (1979) defines a defamatory communication:

> A communication is defamatory if it tends so to harm the reputation of another as to lower him in the estimation of the community or to deter third persons from associating or dealing with him. (p. 375)

Some people mistakenly believe that the truth is an absolute defense to defamation. Persons who work with children and adolescents are generally held to a higher standard than is the average adult in a defamation suit. When a catechist repeats confidential information about a student, the defense of truth may not be sustained because the catechist holds a position of trust and thus can be held to a higher standard than the ordinary person. Catechists must ensure then that opinions and facts concerning students are stated only to those having a right to know.

Any documentation concerning young people must be both accurate and protective of the rights of individuals whose behavior is being described. Records must be objective and factual. Communications should be measured against the standard, "What is written should be specific, behaviorally oriented, and verifiable." It is better to say, "Mary Louise often gazes into space or draws pictures on a note pad during class," than to say, "Mary Louise never pays attention" or "Mary Louise never keeps her mind on the class." The less personal opinion that is stated about a young person, the better.

Slander

Slander, or oral defamation, can arise in seemingly innocent situations. For example, catechist lounge or staff rooms have long been considered safe places in which adults can express themselves freely. As long as the only persons present in the room are catechists and staff members, one may speak without fear of being accused of slander. It is generally held that catechists and staff members are people with a "right to know" one anothers' thoughts and perceptions.

But if other persons, such as visitors, parents, volunteers, maintenance and other workers are present, the staff room is no longer a place for privileged communication. In such a situation, a catechist risks being accused of slander if negative comments are made about young people.

Social gatherings may present other problems. A parent may come to a catechist at a neighborhood party and state, "My son has been spending a great deal of time with Bobby X. I am not so sure that Bobby is a good influence. What is your opinion?" If the catechists responds, "I don't think Bobby is a good influence either," the catechist could be guilty of defamation of character, unprivileged derogatory communication. Catechists should avoid even the appearance of defamatory speech and hence should avoid giving opinions concerning young people to those who have no real right to know those opinions.

Catechists should be extremely prudent in making any comments, whether oral or written, about young people. Comments to parents should be about the parents' own children. Communication should be made only to those persons with a legitimate right to know.

All should remember that a person has a right to reputation. Catechetical leaders and catechists should treat the reputations of those entrusted to their supervision with at least as much care as they would want their own reputations to be treated.

Libel

Libel, written defamation, is generally easier to prove than is slander. Catechists must be sure that the comments made in student records, or in other documents available to persons other than the young person's parents, are based on verifiable occurrences rather than on conjecture.

Questions often arise concerning situations in which catechists are asked to write recommendations for young persons. Obviously, if a catechist wishes to praise a young person, the likelihood that the young person could object is minimal. The problem occurs when a catechist cannot, in conscience, write a favorable recommendation for the young person.

The catechist then has two possible courses of action. He or she can refuse to write a recommendation. No one has an absolute right to a recommendation. Some catechists may feel uncomfortable refusing requests for recommendations, however.

If uncomfortable with the requested recommendation, the catechist may opt for a general letter of reference which does little more than verify that the catechist did indeed instruct the student. The catechist may comment on topics such as concepts studied, activities pursued, etc. This kind of letter says nothing derogatory about a person, although it certainly says nothing very positive, either. The individual receiving the letter should be able to tell that the letter does not constitute an overwhelming endorsement of the young person. Thus, the catechist does not compromise ethics and the student has the minimal documentation needed.

The days when individuals could not see their records are over. In the end, as St. Thomas More once observed, "It is a question of love, not law." If catechists truly love their students, they will not ask, "How can I write so that I won't get sued?" but will ask, "How can I write so that I protect both the reputation of those in my care and my own reputation as a minister who abides by the highest ethical standards?"

CHAPTER 7

Catechist/Student Relationships in Religious Education

C atechists and other staff members care about students. That care extends to all areas of student life. Catechists often find themselves counseling students in personal matters; it is not unusual for a catechist to find him or herself in the position of "surrogate parent" for a student. Students often entrust catechists with confidential information. Catechists, many of whom have little training in professional counseling, often have questions about what is appropriate in interacting with students outside the classroom and/or parish setting. There are few guidelines available; catechists and other personnel may deal with situations that pose personal and legal risks for the adults as well as the students. This author is familiar with several situations in which parents threatened and/or pursued legal action against an educator whose actions they viewed as unwise, inappropriate, sexually motivated, or interfering with the parent/child relationship. Thus, all adults working in the catechetical ministry of the Church should be aware of the legal ramifications involved in student/catechist relationships.

Confidentiality

Most educators rightfully consider student confidences to be sacred. If a student confides in a catechist, the student should be able to presume that the confidential information normally will not be shared with anyone. Educators may believe that they have some type of immunity which protects them from legal liability if they refuse to share student information which was given in confidence.

However, the facts indicate that very few states provide any sort of immunity or privilege for persons who receive confidential information from students. If a catechist were subpoenaed, placed on the stand, and asked for confidential information, most judges would require the catechist to answer. The catechist does not enjoy the type of privilege that doctor/patient, lawyer/client or priest/penitent enjoy.

Another situation that is fairly common involves the student who tells an adult that suicide or other violent action is being considered. Such information must be shared with appropriate persons or the educator can risk being found liable for negligence if injury occurs.

To avoid misunderstanding, catechists should establish the ground rules for confidences early in the relationship. Catechists who require journal writing or other exercises that may involve the sharing of personal feelings should inform the entire class of the rules.

Basically, catechists should honor the confidences of students unless health or safety is involved. In such an instance, the student should know that the greater good requires that the information be revealed. (For further discussion of the issues relating to confidentiality, see also Part 2, Chapter 5: Keeping the Confidences of Young People.)

Sexual Misconduct

One end of the student/catechist relationship spectrum is represented by sexual misconduct. Sexual misconduct *can* be alleged in apparently innocent situations. Students *can* misinterpret touching, and catechists *could* find themselves facing child abuse charges. Extreme caution is in order whenever a catechist touches a student.

Another kind of problem is posed by a student who believes that a catechist has not responded to efforts to achieve a closer relationship. Such a student may accuse a catechist of inappropriate conduct as a retaliatory measure. Educators must be aware that serious consequences can result from an allegation of child abuse, even if that allegation is eventually proven to be false. At the very least, such a false allegation can be extremely embarrassing for the catechist. If a child abuse report is made, the catechist will be questioned by authorities and the investigation will be recorded. In some states, lists of suspected child abusers are kept. Thus, it is imperative that catechists protect themselves and the students they teach by practicing appropriate behavior with students. To avoid even the slightest hint of impropriety, a catechist should avoid being alone with a single student behind closed doors unless a window or other opening permits outsiders to see into the area. A good question to ask one's self might be, "If this were my child, would I have any objection to a catechist relating with him or her in this manner?"

Fear of teachers facing child abuse allegations has caused some public school districts in this country to adopt school rules that prohibit any faculty touching of students. Such rules preclude putting one's arm around students, patting a student on the back, or even giving a student a hug. No catechetical leader would want to take such a position, but common sense precautions must be taken for the protection of all.

Other Physical Contact

Catechists can also be charged with child abuse that is not

sexual. Corporal punishment, which is prohibited by regulation in most Catholic schools, can set the stage for allegations of physical abuse. Corporal punishment can be defined as "any touching that can be construed as punitive." This author is aware of a case in which a teacher tapped a child on the shoulder with a folder while reprimanding the child for not having his homework done. The child's mother filed a child abuse report against the teacher and threatened to file charges of assault and battery. Although this case is outrageous, it does indicate the dangers that can exist. Thus, catechists are well-advised to adopt an operating rule, "Never touch a child in a way that can be construed as punitive."

Other Behaviors

Catechists and other staff members must bear in mind that they are professionals rendering a service. Just as a counselor or psychiatrist is professionally bound to avoid emotional involvement with a client, a catechist should strive to avoid becoming so emotionally involved with a student that objectivity and fairness are compromised. Catechists must remember that they have many students for whom they are responsible and who need and may desire the catechist's attention. If a relationship with a student keeps a catechist from responding to other student needs on a regular basis, the catechist should seriously examine the appropriateness of the relationship.

In seeking to assess the appropriateness of an adult/child relationship, some mental health professionals recommend asking one's self questions such as these: Whose needs are being met? Is there a boundary? Where is it?

The following adult behaviors could be considered inappropriate, depending on the totality of the circumstances:

- dropping by a student's home, particularly if no parent is present
- frequent telephoning of the student
- social trips with a student
- sharing of catechist's personal problems.

Serving as a catechist in these times is a privilege and a gift. It is indeed sad when a catechist is forced to relinquish that gift because of inappropriate choices. Thoughtful reflection and prudent behavior will keep catechists and catechetical leaders both legally protected and professionally fulfilled.

Part 3:
Legal Issues in the Administration of Catechetical Progams

CHAPATER 1

Handbook Development

The development and/or revision of handbooks may well be one of the most important responsibilities facing a catechetical leader. A catechist handbook enables catechists to become familiar with the policies and procedures of the program. A family handbook enables students and parents to understand expectations and responsibilities.

New catechetical leaders may find themselves in a situation in which no handbooks exist or in which existing handbooks are very incomplete, seemingly inappropriate or even at odds with what the new administrator desires to see in the program. Seasoned catechetical leaders may be aware that their handbooks are inadequate and could stand improvement but may be at a loss as to where to begin the process of developing or revising handbooks. The following will suggest areas that could be considered in the formulation of legally sound catechist and family handbooks for the catechetical program.

One helpful technique, keeping a series of index cards, may be employed over a period of time prior to the actual composition and dissemination of handbooks. Every time the catechetical leader thinks of something that should be in the handbook, the item is written on an index card. The catechetical leader may wish to enlist the help of catechists by asking them to submit similar index cards containing any items they believe should be included in the handbook. It is helpful to confine each card to one item only.

Later, the cards can be sorted by categories for inclusion in the handbooks. Such an approach can help the catechetical leader to understand that writing or revising handbooks can be accomplished in steps, rather than in a monumental one-time writing.

There is more than one approach to organizing the contents of a handbook. Some administrators prefer an alphabetical approach. Such an approach can certainly make finding items in a handbook easier. However, a catechetical leader could decide that a topical arrangement is more suitable to a given program's needs.

Catechist/Staff Handbooks

The catechist and/or staff handbook should cover at least the following six areas:
- program philosophy
- instructional duties
- non-instructional duties
- supervision of catechists
- personnel policies
- sample forms.

Each of these area will be discussed in this section.

Program Philosophy/Mission statement

The philosophy or mission statement of the catechetical program should be the basis for all policies and procedures. Ideally, the life of the program should be seen as flowing from the philosophy or mission statement. Basically, the catechetical program philosophy or mission statement answers the question, "What do we say that we are doing in this parish program?"

Rules and regulations should be consistent with the stated philosophy or mission of the program. It is important, therefore, that rules and proposed rule changes be reviewed in the light of the philosophy or mission statement.

Generally parishes and catechetical programs already have a philosophy or mission statement. It is a good idea to review the philosophy or mission statement at least once a year in order to evaluate the program's performance. Areas of significant disagreement should be settled, so that each year the catechists can "own" the philosophy or mission statement and the policies and procedures which emanate from it. The philosophy or mission statement should be a help in the development of all policies and procedures.

Instructional duties

At first glance, it might appear that instructional duties should occupy the bulk of the handbook. Certainly, those duties are the ones that are uppermost in the minds of catechetical leaders and catechists. The first area under this section should deal with what catechists are expected to do in the instruction of young people. It is not necessary to dictate *how* catechists are to do everything, but it is necessary to delineate some broad guidelines as to *what* they are to accomplish.

A second area might be called "Supervision of Students" within the learning situation. Supervision outside the regular instructional situation would be discussed under non-teaching duties. The responsibilities of catechists for students in the classroom should be thoroughly discussed. The fact that supervision is mental (the person has to be paying attention to the students) as well as physical (the person is bodily present) should be stressed. Emergency procedures should be addressed.

A third area would deal with the records that should be kept concerning student attendance and performance. It is important that catechists keep careful records indicating which students were absent on each occasion. It is not uncommon for courts to request this type of information even years after a student has left a program. Often diocesan policies establish the norms for the length of time catechetical records should be retained. In the absence of such policies, check with diocesan officials regarding the norms in your state.

Non-Instructional duties

While catechists or other staff members may believe that their only task is to provide religious instruction, they do have other responsibilities to the program. A catechetical leader might want to utilize the index card method and begin writing down everything a catechist is expected to do that is not, strictly speaking, an instructional duty. Even if the catechetical program has a handbook, a catechetical leader might find that a week of keeping "non-instructional duties" in mind is a worthwhile exercise.

One area of non-instructional duties comes immediately to mind. Catechists and other staff members should be reminded that their duties do not begin and end with the classroom. If a student is in the hallway when he or she should be in class, for example, the catechist who learns of this situation needs to report it. If students are "fooling around" and/or presenting other problems before programs start, the catechist needs to address the behavior.

Student behavior codes should be printed in the catechist handbook, even if they are printed in a separate handbook for parents and/or students, so that catechists have all policies and procedures readily accessible in one place.

Off-site activities should be addressed. Procedures for supervising retreats and service programs should be explained.

Expectations for catechist attendance at parent meetings and catechist gatherings should also be stated. Even though a staff may be comprised largely of volunteers, both catechists and staff members have responsibilities for the success of the program and the safety of students. The wise catechetical leader will not shrink from holding catechists accountable.

Supervision and evaluation of catechists

Catechetical leaders have a responsibility to supervise and evaluate catechists. Practically, this means that the catechetical leader will visit classrooms. Catechists should understand that they will be supervised. The format for supervisory visits and the follow-up expected should be addressed.

Personnel policies for catechists

While catechists are generally not paid employees, there are some personnel issues that should be addressed. For example, how does a catechist notify a catechetical leader that he or she will not be available for a given session? Who is responsible for obtaining a substitute?

It is important that catechists be persons of good moral character. There should be some statement about the expectation that catechists will live a life that is consistent with the teachings of the Catholic Church.

Sample forms

A final area that should be included in catechist handbooks involves sample forms. These forms will, of course, differ from program to program. It is certainly more practical and efficient to have all forms located in one place. Whatever forms are used — permission forms, progress reports, accident forms, etc. should be included. Such a procedure ensures that all catechists know what the "official" forms are and have easy access to them.

Summary

The six areas of philosophy, instructional duties, non-instructional duties, supervision of catechists, personnel policies and sample forms are crucial in the development of a catechist handbook. There are other areas that may be included and which may be important to a given program.

There is no one right or wrong way to compose a catechist handbook. Each catechetical leader has to decide what is important for his or her catechists. The above is simply a discussion of six areas which ought to be included in some way in every catechist handbook. The points discussed should give catechetical leaders some "food for thought" as they develop or revise their handbooks.

The six components discussed are broad areas of concern. More experienced catechetical leaders may already have legally sound catechist handbooks in place. As new concerns arise, the catechetical leader and other appropriate parties will develop policies and regulations to meet the new concerns. Sometimes this kind of reactive approach is unavoidable. Certainly, a proactive approach which attempts to envision possible difficulties is preferable to trying to develop a policy to meet a problem as it arises, and seeking to minimize future problems by developing policy after problems arise.

Family Handbooks

A catechetical program needs to ensure that both parents and students understand the rules and policies of the program and parish and agree to be governed by those rules and policies. Some catechetical programs have separate handbooks for parents and students. This author believes that having one handbook for both parents and students is preferable to having separate handbooks. The catechetical leader should ask parents to discuss the handbook with their children. In this way, families are able to participate as a unit in the life of the catechetical program and parish. Parents share the responsibility for their children's understanding the philosophy of the program and the rules that flow from that philosophy. Parents and students should be asked to sign a statement that they have read and discussed the handbook and that they agree to support its provisions.

When catechetical leaders and other administrators consider handbooks, rules and regulations come to mind. Most administrators and attorneys would agree that the best law is, like medicine, preventive. The best defense is having tried to follow the right course in the first place. All catechetical leaders must look carefully at their rules and procedures to be confident that they are reasonable, fair and consistent.

In any disagreement involving parents or students that results in a lawsuit, courts will look for evidence of good faith: Did the program have a rule that was promulgated? Did the student or parent know of the rule? Courts do not concern themselves with the rightness or wrongness of the professional opinion of educators. A court is only concerned with the existence of a properly promulgated rule and with staff acting in good faith according to the procedures it stated would be followed.

Catechetical leaders must understand that they will never be able to write down everything a student might possibly do that could result in sanctions. Therefore it is advisable to have some kind of "catch-all" clause such as "other inappropriate conduct." No court will expect a program administrator to have stated all possible offenses, but courts will expect that something is in writing and that students and parents have a reasonable idea of the expectations of the parish and/or program.

All adults involved in catechetical programs must be concerned with being models of mature, responsible, Christian behavior. Policies and procedures must be examined in the light of responsible behavior.

As in the construction of catechist handbooks, the beginning point for rule development should be the philosophy/mission statement of the program or parish which is available to all members of the community. Even first graders can be brought to some understanding of the philosophy/mission statement: "At St. Michael's, we try to treat each other the way Jesus would want." The life of the parish should be seen as flowing from the mission statement.

Rules are just one more facet of life and should carry out the philosophy/mission statement. For example, it would seem inconsistent with a philosophy promoting the development of mature Christian persons to state, "Absences from catechetical programs will not be excused without a doctor's note." Such a rule, besides being unreasonable, would preclude provisions for other necessary absences, such as attendance at funerals, etc.

Rules should be clear and understandable. The test that might be applied by the courts would be the following: Would two persons of average intelligence reading this rule have the same understanding of it? A rule stating, "Students arriving at class after the bell has rung will be marked tardy" is clear while a rule such as "Late students will be marked tardy" is open to such questions as: How late is late? after the bell? after the catechist begins the lesson?

Whenever possible, rules should be written as there are certainly common sense reasons for writing rules. When emotions run high, it is easier to pick up the written rule than to insist that "at the beginning of the year you were told thus and such."

Having a written handbook should encourage the catechetical leader to strive for clarity in rule-making. Periodic evaluation would enable the program to make necessary changes. The following discussion highlights major areas that might be considered in the development of a family handbook.

Philosophy/Mission statement

As stated throughout this chapter, the philosophy/mission statement is basic and should be included in all handbooks. Every member of the community and, indeed all who come into contact with the catechetical program should see that persons are striving to live out the philosophy which governs the parish or school.

Admission policies

This section should discuss the qualifications and procedures for admission. Some examples of questions that should be addressed are: Do students have to be members of the sponsoring parish to attend? What prerequisites are involved? For example, does a student have to be baptized? Must a student have received First Communion before entering Confirmation preparation, regardless of student age?

Program policies

This section of the handbook may deal with parish or diocesan policies regarding catechetical programs. What level of parental involvement or attendance at parent meetings is expected or required?

What are parents expected to do to monitor the attendance and participation of their children in the program?

What kind of records are kept? How long are attendance and disciplinary records kept? Who has access to these?

The rights of non-custodial parents should be included here. Legal precedent suggests that parents do not cease to be parents when they no longer have custody of their children. Therefore, catechetical leaders may wish to include a statement in the handbook such as:

> This parish catechetical program abides by the provisions of the Buckley Amendment with respect to the rights of non-custodial parents. In the absence of a court order to the contrary, we will provide the non-custodial parent with unofficial copies of records. If there is a court order specifying that there is to be no information given, it is the responsibility of the custodial parent to provide the catechetical leader with an official copy of the court order.

Another way to handle the non-custodial parent situation is to ask all divorced parents to furnish the catechetical leader with a court-certified copy of the custody section of the divorce decree. This information will also help the administrator determine when, if ever, a child can be released to a non-custodial parent.

Communication

Many problems can be avoided if the handbook states the procedures by which parents contact program catechists and staff, and they in turn contact parents.

In keeping with the Church's principle of subsidiarity, problems should be solved at the lowest level whenever possible. Thus, it would seem advisable that persons having a problem with an individual go directly to that person before going to that person's superior. If a parent has a complaint about a catechist, it seems only just that the parent discuss the difficulty first with the catechist. If the parent is reluctant to confront the catechist alone, the catechetical leader might offer to be present at the conference. Requiring persons to attempt to work out their difficulties mutually is certainly consistent with the demands of the Gospel and makes good legal sense as well.

If a parent wishes to communicate with a catechist, how should contact be made? How should a parent contact the catechetical leader? If an appointment is necessary, how should it be made? Obviously, there are times when informal contacts will occur. There are also times when everyone will profit if people have an opportunity to distance themselves from the situation before discussing it. Thus, the existence of a procedure for communication can be helpful.

Behavioral expectations

As this chapter has indicated, the catechetical leader should strive for simplicity and clarity in rule construction; long lists of rules should probably be avoided. Phrases such as "other inappropriate behavior" or "conduct unbecoming a Christian student" cover many types of misbehavior. Examples of infractions could be provided.

Phrases such as "must" or "result in a certain penalty" can result in little or no leeway. Phrases such as "can" or "may" give a catechetical leader room to allow for individual circumstances.

There should be some avenue for an appeal or the stating of a grievance. Generally, the pastor would be the next person contacted if the parent is not satisfied with the action taken by a catechetical leader.

Off-Site activities

The types of off-site activities, such as retreats and field trips, should be discussed. If service programs are required, they should be described. Permission forms should be included in the handbook, as well as given to students prior to the trip or activity.

Use of parish grounds and facilities

The problems of students arriving very early for a program or staying long after a program's end must be addressed. The appropriate times for student presence should be listed, and penalties for non-compliance should be stated.

(At the same time, the catechetical leader must understand that a student should never be left alone on parish property, even if it means the catechetical leader or another adult must stay with the child.)

Right to amend

No matter how proactive a catechetical leader is, situations will arise that were not foreseen. The catechetical leader should retain the right to amend the handbook for just cause and should state that parents will be given prompt notification if changes are made.

Agreements signed by parents and students

For everyone's protection, parents and students should be required to sign a statement such as, "We have read and agree to be governed by this handbook." Such a statement avoids many of the problems that can arise when parents or students state that they did not know a certain rule existed.

A catechetical leader would be well advised not to admit a young person to the program until such a signed agreement is submitted. Since courts can construe handbooks as contracts, it is both legally and ethically wise to ensure that all parties to the contract have read it and agree to be ruled by it.

A Concluding Thought

While the development of handbooks may appear to be simply one more task for an already busy catechetical leader, sound handbooks can contribute greatly to the smooth operation of a program. When everyone understands rights and responsibilities, everyone profits.

CHAPTER 2

Boards of Religious Education

The years since the second Vatican Council have witnessed an ever-increasing role for the laity in the Church, especially in Catholic education. Membership on a religious education board, or on an education commission responsible for total Catholic education, is one way that the laity share in the catechetical ministry of the Church. At no time in our history has the role of the board been more important than it is now. What board members do is crucial to the mission of catechesis and total Catholic education.

Good board members are invaluable. Catechetical leaders and pastors want them; parishes and dioceses need them. Generous, qualified people are usually forthcoming. But these people have a need and a right to know the legal implications of their membership on boards. Too many lawsuits involving the Catholic Church have reached the courts and made the front pages. Board members should be concerned. Questions frequently asked are "What are my legal responsibilities? For what can I be held personally liable? Does the parish or diocese have liability insurance that will protect board members? Can I be sued as an individual for actions of the board?". These are intelligent questions and people should ask them before committing themselves to board membership. State laws vary but generally, members of not-for-profit boards will not be held liable for good faith actions. It is important to check with diocesan officials regarding board member responsibilities within your state.

Canon, or Church law, also governs Catholic religious education. Catechetical leaders and board members have no authority to act outside the provisions of canon law. But within the provisions of canon law, there is great freedom so long as no civil laws are broken.

Models for Boards

There are currently two main models for boards of religious education: *consultative boards* and *boards with limited jurisdiction*. In the past, terms such as advisory and policy-making have been used. For the sake of consistency, the terms *consultative* and *boards with limited jurisdiction* will be used.

Consultative board

A consultative board is one generally established by the pastor or by diocesan policy. This board has responsibilities for the development and/or approval of policies. The pastor, or the bishop in the case of a diocesan board, has the final authority to accept the recommendations of a consultative board. It would seem that the consultative model would be most effective if the pastor and catechetical leader be members of the board and be in regular attendance at meetings. This would help to insure that the canon law principles of collegiality would function. If the pastor and catechetical leader are not in regular attendance, the board members could view themselves as functioning in a vacuum. If the pastor regularly decides not to follow the decisions of the board, members could view their role as useless.

Thus, even though such a consultative board is strictly speaking, advisory, everyone's best interests are served if the board is able to use a consensus model of decision-making whenever possible. Consensus does not necessarily mean that everyone agrees that a certain action is the best possible action or that it reflects one's personal preference. Rather, consensus means that all members have agreed to support the decision for the sake of the ministry. For example, a board member might personally have selected a different candidate than the one chosen if the board member had sole responsibility for appointing the catechetical leader. Because other board members prefer a given candidate, the board member agrees to support that candidate. It is important to note that consensus does not mean that the minority agrees to go along with the majority. It means that all members can support a decision. Sometimes, the majority will support the choice of the minority if it is clear that the minority, in all good conscience, cannot support the action that the majority favors.

Boards with limited jurisdiction

A board with limited jurisdiction has been defined by NCEA publications as one "constituted by the pastor to govern the parish education program, subject to certain decisions which are reserved to the pastor and the bishop". This type of board would have, in both theory and practice, more autonomy in decision making than would the consultative board because the pastor has delegated decision-making power to the board with limited jurisdiction. Pastors and bishops can delegate power, but they cannot delegate their ultimate responsibility for actions taken in their parishes or dioceses. The responsibility of a superior for the actions of those under him or her has roots in civil law as well as in canon law. The civil law doctrine of *respondeat superior* requires that a superior must answer for the actions of a subordinate. Generally, if a board is sued for its actions, the pastor and the bishop will be sued as well. Canon law requires that any ministry wishing to call itself Catholic have the permission and recognition of the bishop. Traditionally, all programs must be subject to the bishop in matters of faith and morals. Canon law requires that the bishop exercise supervision over the religious education programs of parishes and those who teach in such programs. Board members, therefore, must understand and accept the bishops' authority in these matters; to attempt to act in a manner contrary to the wishes of the bishop could place the parish and its religious education program's continuation at risk.

Current Practice

Many consultative boards function like boards with limited jurisdiction. The present movement towards government by collegiality and consensus sometimes results in little, if any, formal vote-taking. Therefore in practice, it is often difficult to distinguish between consultative boards and boards with limited jurisdiction.

Religious education boards have an important role. It is crucial that board members understand that power is vested in the board as a body, not in individual members. Board members must understand what the role of the board is — the development of policy. Even if the policies have to be approved at a higher level, board members must understand their role in terms of policy.

Policy Development

Policy is usually defined as a guide for discretionary action. Thus, policy will dictate what the board wishes to be done. Policy is not concerned with administration or implementation; that is, the board should not become involved in *how* its directives will be implemented or with the specific persons who will implement them. For example, the board might adopt a policy requiring the parents of First Communicants and those being confirmed to attend parent education programs. When and where such programs are held, how long each session lasts, and how many sessions are required should not be determined by the board. Such questions are administrative ones; they are to be dealt with by the catechetical leader who is the chief executive officer of the program. Administrative decisions are the day-to-day management choices of the catechetical leader. It is important for everyone to understand these distinctions from the beginning.

Generally, boards will set policies in at least these major areas: program, finance and personnel. Board members, therefore, need to know the broad parameters of the law as it affects religious education.

The purpose of this chapter is to provide the information which catechetical leaders should make available to prospective and current Catholic religious education board members — basic information concerning canon law and civil law as it impacts religious education. A court would probably expect that a person who accepts membership on a board would have some rudimentary understanding of the laws that apply to the Church and its ministries.

Board Supervision of Programs and Activities

One important duty of boards of religious education is the development of policies that protect the safety of children and adolescents. Board members have a fiduciary duty to persons participating in religious education programs. A fiduciary is one who is entrusted with something belonging to another, and he or she is expected to take more care of the other person's interests than would be taken if the action concerned his or her personal interests. The interest in religious education programs is young people. Thus, it is absolutely essential that the greatest possible attention and care be given to all areas that impact student life, instruction, and well-being.

A common legal standard judging cases involving negligent supervision is, "The younger the child chronologically or mentally, the greater the standard of care." Thus, greater attention should be paid to programs involving the youngest children. Board members will not, of course, be responsible for actual supervision. But boards are responsible for seeing that appropriate policies and procedures for supervision are in place and are being implemented.

In developing policies for supervision, the board member must keep in mind the reasonableness standard and ask, "Is this what one would expect a reasonable person in a similar situation to do?" No one is expected to think of every possible situation that might occur, but reasonable persons can assume that certain situations and/or areas might be potentially dangerous. The best defense for a board in a negligence suit is a reasonable attempt to provide for the safety of those entrusted to its care by the development and implementation of rules and policies. The reasonable board is one that ensures that the catechetical leader supervises catechists in their implementation of rules and policies.

Duties and Responsibilities of Board Members

Obviously, board members have responsibilities to the parish that operates the religious education program. Those duties will usually be found in the Constitution or by-laws of the board. Generally, a board would approve the budget, endorse programs, and establish hiring procedures for paid staff as well as guidelines for selecting and dismissing volunteers. Depending on whether the board was a consultative board or a board with limited jurisdiction, another party such as a parish council, a pastor or group of pastors, may have final approval of all policies suggested by a board.

The board would monitor the programs, the budget and the implementation of policy. The Director of Religious Education would certainly suggest policies and would perhaps write the first drafts of policies. The board would approve the policies (passing them to another party, eg. the pastor, for final approval, as appropriate) and would hold the catechetical leader accountable for their implementation. The board should, therefore, also develop a plan for the evaluation of the catechetical leader's job performance, clearly identifying the role of both the pastor and the board in the evaluation process.

Duties to the diocese/church

The board has definite duties to the diocese and to the larger Church. The board must ensure that the policies it develops are consistent with ones already established by the diocese. If, for example, diocesan policy states that only Catholics who actively practice their religion in accordance with the teaching of the Church may be catechists, the local religious education board must ensure that its policies are consistent with those of the diocese. Practically speaking, this would mean that divorced Catholics who have contracted a second marriage without the Church's approval are not selected as catechists. Boards may be very reluctant to dictate such a policy. However, board members must realize that many injustices are wrought when policies and rules are applied inconsistently or when a local board attempts to act at variance with diocesan policy.

If the board or an individual board member cannot agree with a given diocesan policy, then change must be sought through the appropriate channels. A board is not free to adopt a policy at variance with established diocesan policy. The board's responsibility is clear: to uphold the policies of the diocese and to develop local policies which are in harmony with those of the diocese.

The one non-negotiable area would be that of faith and morals. Any parish program exists under the primary authority of the bishop and so is subject to him in the area of faith and morals. A parish program can never be completely independent of the bishop.

If a local board acts in a manner inconsistent with existing diocesan policy, it is unfair to expect diocesan support if problems result from the board action. When tensions arise, board members must keep their responsibilities to the diocese and to the Church in view. If a board member cannot support a policy (and support does not necessarily mean agreement; it does mean a willingness to live with and not criticize the decision), then the board member's only real choice is to resign from the board.

Duties to the catechetical leader

Boards have responsibilities to the catechetical leader. Today many boards appoint the catechetical leader with the approval of the pastor. If the board does not appoint the catechetical leader, it probably has a significant part in the selection process. The board's first responsibility is to ensure that the person selected meets the qualifications set by the diocese or sponsoring party.

Since the catechetical leader is responsible to the board as well as to other appropriate parties such as the pastor, the catechetical leader should report to the board how he or she is ensuring that policies are implemented. The board should annually review the criteria and procedures for the evaluation of the catechetical leader's job performance. It should further ensure that evaluation (at least the board's part of the process) is, in fact, being conducted according to policy. If evaluation is omitted or done casually, problems can result when a board later attempts to call a catechetical leader to accountability and/or begins to consider non-renewal of contract. It is certainly not moral, and it may well be a breach of contract for a board to vote for non-renewal or recommendation of non-renewal of a catechetical leader's contract without having given the catechetical leader some evaluative feedback and a chance to correct any deficiencies.

The catechetical leader has the right to expect that the administration of the religious education program is his or her responsibility and that board members will not interfere in the day-to-day running of the religious education program. It is often easy for a board member to succumb to the temptation to get involved in disciplinary matters, content disputes, and/or catechist/catechetical leader problems. The board member has to remember that his or her responsibilities are really twofold:

- to develop policies
- to support the persons and activities that implement those policies.

If the board really cannot support the catechetical leader's decisions, the board should call an executive session — one in which no one other than pastor, board members, and catechetical leader are in attendance. In that session, board members can state their views and listen to those of the catechetical leader. Goals and objectives are ways of implementing policies. The catechetical leader may be able to make modifications that would be acceptable to the board. Ideally, the board and the catechetical leader can come to some understanding and/or compromise. If no compromise can be reached that both parties can support, the board may have to call in an outside facilitator or arbitrator.

Disagreements should be left in the board room. Board members must constantly remember that their power is that of the board when it is in session. There is no power vested in individual board members. Becoming involved in catechetical leader/parent or catechist/parent or catechetical leader/catechist disputes only weakens the authority of both the catechetical leader and the board. The catechetical leader however, should keep board members informed about problem or potential problem situations so that board members will be able to respond in an intelligent manner if they are questioned.

There is no more crucial relationship for the success of the ministry of religious education than that of the board and the catechetical leader. That relationship should foster a sound experience in a Christian community. When the catechetical leader and the board function in an atmosphere in which each respects the rights of the other and in which healthy dialogue and the resolution of differences are promoted, the teaching ministry of the Church should thrive.

Duties to catechists

The board does have responsibilities to the catechists. All religious education programs should have catechist/staff handbooks. The catechetical leader is the person who is probably best equipped to make recommendations about what should be in the handbook. The board should approve the handbook as policy. This procedure protects everyone. It is a built-in system of checks and balances. If the catechetical leader is very far afield, board members can tactfully suggest another approach or policy. Catechist/staff handbooks range in size from a few pages stapled together to books of many pages, depending on the size and complexity of the program. At the very minimum, catechist handbooks should contain an outline of expectations regarding instructional duties. These expectations should involve such areas as the construction of lesson plans, homework policies and evaluation standards. Non-instructional duties should also be addressed. Generally, these duties are more controversial than instructional duties. Such requirements as hall and playground supervision should be discussed. The procedures to be followed for off-site trips should be detailed. If an unfortunate accident were to occur on a trip and no specific policies were in place, a catechist or other supervising adult could rightfully claim that the board was at fault for failing to ensure that proper procedures were followed. (See also Part 3, Chapter 1: Handbook Development)

If the parish or the diocese does not have a grievance procedure governing religious education programs, the local board should begin developing one to ensure that all are treated fairly. A grievance procedure should provide a mechanism through which problems can be settled at the lowest possible level. The first step might be to discuss the problem informally with the catechetical leader. A second step could be a committee of the board. Third, the whole board could consider the grievance. The pastor should be the last avenue of appeal before the bishop. What constitutes matter for a grievance should be clearly stated. Every disagreement a person has with a catechetical leader is not a potential grievance. Only serious situations which cannot be solved through other channels should be brought to a grievance procedure.

Duties to the parent/student community

A fourth group to which the board has specific responsibilities is the parent/student community. All religious education programs should have a parent/student handbook in which the policies that affect parents and students are explained. Some areas that should be included are:

- admission policies
- program content policies
- the procedure for communication between parents and catechists and/or the catechetical leader
- the discipline code
- rules concerning off-site activities
- field trip policies and forms
- emergency procedures
- parent service and fund-raising requirements
- the role of the religious education board.

Parents should be informed about the function of the religious education board and about the policies governing attendance at board meetings, speaking at board meetings, and bringing matters to the attention of the board. Religious education boards must guard against becoming a "dumping ground" for complaints. Only serious matters which appropriately belong before the board should be considered and then, only after all other channels have been exhausted. Boards should not become involved in matters which are the province of catechist or catechetical leader.

Board members have serious responsibilities to the Church, to the diocese, to the parish or parishes that sponsor the program, to the catechetical leader, to catechists and staff, and to parents and students. The role of the board member is to oversee good program operation and effective ministry through the development of sound policy.

Conclusion and recommendations

Religious education board members should familiarize themselves with the law as it affects private, religious institutions. Since religious education board members are responsible for the development of policies, familiarity with law will be most helpful. Religious education board members should be cognizant of the principles of law involved in landmark court decisions and should be able to understand the courts' reasoning; in so doing, board members should be able to apply the appropriate concepts to their own policy making.

Although religious education programs are not bound by all the constraints that public sector programs are, knowledge of those constraints should aid the religious education board member in developing policies that are fair and equitable. Just because a religious education program is not legally bound to do something does not mean that the thing should not be done if it seems the morally right thing to do. Boards of religious education should always be concerned with respecting the dignity of catechetical leaders, catechists, other staff members, parents and students as human beings. When contemplating a possible course of action, one should ask if that is really the fair thing to do? Is it moral? Is this what I would want or expect someone to do to me if I were in the position?

One of the best recommendations that could be made to religious education board members is to strive always to act in a manner that is respectful of the dignity, rights and safety of all those in the religious education program.

Due Process

Although religious education programs are not required to follow constitutional due process procedures, there is much to be learned from the public sector in this area. It seems that the Gospel would demand that at least the minimum requirements of due process be afforded to those in religious education programs. It would also seem wise, ethical and within the dictates of common sense to grant a minimum of due process.

Justice and common sense would indicate that religious education programs should strive towards reasonable fairness, if not towards constitutional due process. The rudiments of due process should be met in any conflict: notice and hearing before an impartial tribunal. The courts have indicated that private institutions can be held to a standard of fundamental reasonableness, and it is by that standard (as well as the Gospel) that religious education programs should seek to judge actions, whether or not court action ever becomes a reality.

A Final Note

The development of private sector law has been slower than the development of public sector law. Yet, no longer can parishes expect the judicial restraint that kept courts from intervening in the past. Courts are holding all private parties to a standard of fairness.

Parishes and parish programs *formerly* found almost absolute immunity from successful litigation in the doctrine of separation of church and state. Cases arising over the last several years indicate, however, that courts can and will intervene in non-doctrinal aspects of a private institution's operation.

Catechetical leaders and board members can no longer afford to be ignorant of the law as it pertains to them and to their institutions. Ignorance can prove costly both in terms of finance, time, and the failure to model Gospel values. Study of law can provide catechetical leaders and board members with the knowledge and the tools needed to avoid being sued.

Justice and common sense seem to demand that religious education members, striving to be faithful to the mission and philosophy of their parishes, would seek knowledge of private sector law. In the final analysis, each person — board member, pastor, catechetical leader, catechist — has to answer to his or her conscience. The law is a kind of watchdog over the behavior of persons. Religious education board members have been given a great trust, and if they possess wider latitude in governing their programs than do their public sector counterparts, it seems that their responsibilities are also greater.

Jesus' plea for integrity in the lives of his disciples is, perhaps, the best advice that a religious education board member could ponder: "For what will it profit them if they gain the whole world but forfeit their life? Or what will they give in return for their life?" (Matt. 16:26) Fidelity to their own highest principles and to Gospel calls should insure that religious education board members remain well within the parameters of law, both divine and human.

CHAPTER 3

Contracts and the Law: Who is Protected?

The prevailing law in Catholic institutions and other private institutions is contract law. A contract is an agreement be tween two parties who both "incur detriments" and "derive benefits" from the contract.

A catechetical leader agrees to administer a religious education program, a "detriment" in that one is unable to perform other employment during that time, and the person hired receives a "benefit" (salary, etc.). The parish also incurs a "detriment" (payment of salary) and a "benefit" (its parishioners are receiving religious education).

One might be tempted to believe that, since most catechists receive no pay for their services, contracts are not involved. However, the benefit does not have to be a monetary one. One could make a case that conferring the title of catechist on a person and considering that individual as a member of the catechetical staff are benefits to the catechist and a legal detriment to the parish in that other persons cannot have the position which the catechist holds. While such reasoning may appear to be something of a "stretch," it is important for parishes and catechetical leaders to construct an agreement that confers benefits and makes demands on the catechist. Far too many people believe that since catechists are largely volunteers, they cannot be held to any requirements. Such a belief is inaccurate and is an insult to the person giving his or her time as a catechist. Surely, if what the catechist is doing is important (and what is more important than the catechesis of parishioners?), the catechist will expect to be held to standards of behavior and performance. To dispense with such standards is, in effect, indicating that what the catechist does is not important to the life and well-being of the parish.

Parents and Students as Contracting Parties

According to Canon law, religious education is a right of all parishioners, but it is not an absolute right. It is possible for a young person or an adult to behave in such a manner that the right is forfeited. The parish in effect, enters into a contract with the parents of young people. The parish agrees to provide religious education and the parents agree to see that their children come to classes or activities and behave in an appropriate manner. It is advisable to put the contractual understanding in writing and to have both parents and young persons sign the agreement, if possible. Legally, a person under the age of eighteen cannot enter into a contract, but it is a good idea to remind young persons of their responsibilities as members of the parish and the religious education community.

Breach of Contract

Breach of contract occurs when one party fails to perform. When a parish is involved in litigation with personnel or members, the court will examine the provisions of the contract. *Weithoff v. St. Veronica School,* 210 N.W. 2d 108 (Mich. 1973,) an early — but significant case illustrates. The parish terminated Weithoff's contract as a teacher after her marriage to a priest who had not been laicized. She had signed a contract of employment which bound her to observe the "promulgated" policies of the sponsoring parish. A policy requiring teachers to be practicing Catholics had been adopted by the governing body, but the policy was filed and never published to employees. Therefore, Ms. Weithoff alleged that the school's dismissal of her was a breach of contract. The court agreed and ordered the parish to pay damages, since the remedy for breach of contract in the private sector is damages, not reinstatement.

Weithoff illustrates the importance of contract language. Had there been no clause requiring "promulgation," there is a strong possibility that the school would have won this case. The court might well have maintained that a person who teaches in a Catholic school should expect to be held to the requirements of Church law.

Breach of contract can be committed by either party to the contract — the parish or the employee. It is generally conceded however, that it is futile for a private institution to bring breach of contract charges against an employee who wants to terminate a contract. To compel a person to work would be tantamount to involuntary servitude. Courts have stated that since replacements are readily available, a private entity sustains no injury. Without an injury, there can be no lawsuit. As frustrating as this reality can be for parishes, it is simply a fact of life.

Young Persons and Breach: Suspension of Students

There are virtually no cases in courts of record involving allegations of church failure to provide religious education to young persons. However, the present state of litigation certainly leads one to expect that such litigation may be forthcoming.

The use of student/parent handbooks and the requirement that parents and young persons sign an agreement that they "have read and agree to abide by the provisions of the handbook," will do much to ensure an effective program and compliance with reasonable rules and regulations.

One area that has resulted in concern in parish communities is that of the suspended or dismissed participant. While suspension and dismissal may seem like harsh actions to take in a parish catechetical program, they are sometimes necessary. When a student consistently violates program rules and does not respond to efforts to correct behavior, he or she may need to be removed from the program for a period of time. The young person needs to understand that certain behaviors will not be tolerated. Indeed such a lesson is a good preparation for life. The rights of other students must be respected also. A disruptive student denies others the catechesis to which they are entitled.

Due Process: Fairness Considerations

In the public sector due process demands that an accused person be given notice and a hearing before an impartial tribunal. Further, the accused has the right to question accusers, to provide witnesses, to have an attorney present, and to appeal the decision. Recently many courts are requiring at least the first three elements (*notice* and a *hearing* before *an impartial tribunal*) as essential components of basic contractual fairness in the non-public sector. At minimum, directors of catechetical programs should develop policies requiring that a young person facing suspension or dismissal and his or her parents be told of the charges and be given an opportunity to refute them. Some process for appeal should be in place. The pastor should be available as a reviewer of disciplinary action taken. In most dioceses, the bishop is the "last court of appeal."

Conclusion

Catechetical programs are not bound by constitutional due process but they are bound by common law considerations of fundamental fairness. Further, the Gospel demands that those in authority treat others as Jesus would.

Parish boards of religious education/ Catholic education commissions should carefully develop and review policies concerning discipline of young persons in catechetical programs. (See also Part 3, Chapter 2: Boards of Religious Education.) Reasons for dismissal should be listed. Sometimes it is difficult to balance legal and Gospel considerations when developing and implementing policies, but such is the challenge facing catechetical leaders.

CHAPTER 4

Documentation of Catechist/Staff Behaviors: What Should Your Document? How Should You Document?

C atechetical leaders often ask questions concerning written documentation of catechist and/or student behavior. Twenty years ago it was rare to find much written documentation. Administrators often expressed a belief that little or no documentation was good, since it gave a person a second chance. Today, increasing litigation demonstrates that such a belief is not good operational theory. On the contrary, documentation is an absolute necessity in protecting both institutions and administrators; good documentation also ensures that everyone's rights are protected. This chapter will address some of the main issues in documentation, and will offer a model for good record keeping.

Contracts and Related Documents

The catechist/staff handbook should state, at least in general terms, the expectations for behavior. It is unfair for a catechist to be told, after the fact, that certain behavior is unacceptable if there are no standards, or if standards are vague. Obviously, there are some behaviors which everyone ought to know are unacceptable, such as theft, dishonesty, etc.

The catechist handbook should also indicate what behaviors can result in dismissal. Some persons mistakenly believe that "volunteers cannot be fired." The important factor to keep in mind in any such situation is documentation. The best protection against a successful lawsuit is a written record of the reasons and events leading to dismissal.

Some behaviors fall into "gray" areas. For example, what is inappropriate behavior with students? What is sexual harassment? Can it be sexual harassment if the person is joking? (Answer: yes. See also Part 1, Chapter 5: Sexual Harassment))

When a catechetical leader believes that a catechist has done something unacceptable, the administrator should ask whether the parish or program's documents make it clear that such behavior is inappropriate. If there is any possibility that a reasonable person might not have known that such an action was prohibited, the administrator should: give the person the benefit of the doubt; advise that such behavior is not acceptable, and that any such subsequent behavior will be documented; and immediately take steps to ensure that all catechists and staff are made aware of expectations.

In the event that the behavior of a catechist is undesirable or ineffective, the catechetical leader should document all events that illustrate what it is that has given cause for concern. Administrators should keep in mind that catechists may be doing an adequate job teaching but may still be behaving outside the classroom in ways that are unacceptable. Some examples might be: excessive absenteeism or tardiness, lack of cooperation, criticizing parish/Church officials to students, etc. All documentation should be written in language that is specific, behaviorally-oriented, and verifiable. It would be better to record, "Mr. Thompson sent twenty students to the office in a three-week period," than to state, "Mr. Thompson is having difficulty keeping order."

In cases in which catechist behavior does not meet administrative expectations, the catechetical leader or other supervisor should have a "paper trail" indicating that the individual was told of problems and given an opportunity to improve. One way to ensure appropriate communication and documentation is to follow a seven-point checklist when meeting with catechists or other staff members who present problems.

Checklist for Conferencing With Catechists and Staff

The following checklist can be used in drafting a document which is presented to the catechist or staff member and in conducting the actual conference. These steps can also be followed in conferencing with employed staff in the catechetical program setting such as a secretary.

1. Enumerate precisely what is wrong and needs improvement.

> Because it is difficult to correct other adults, administrators may fall into the trap of speaking too generally. The catechist or staff member may not know exactly what he or she did that was not acceptable and may not understand what new behavior(s) are expected.

2. State that the parish wants the individual to improve.

Such a statement indicates good faith on the part of the administrator, and can be most important in any subsequent litigation.

3. State what the administrator is going to do to help.

A beginning catechist could be assigned a more experienced catechist as a mentor who could advise in matters of instruction and classroom management. A catechist could also be sent to another parish for a professional day/evening experience of observing catechists with proven records of good teaching and discipline. A catechist or staff member with personal problems could be referred to a counselor.

4. Give a deadline at which time all parties will review improvement or lack thereof.

If no deadline is given and maintained, a person could later claim, "I never heard back from you so I assumed everything was all right." Thus, it is absolutely imperative that the administrator give time parameters, such as two weeks, a month, two months. A date and time for a follow-up meeting should be established before the end of the conference.

5. State that, if there is no improvement within the time frame stated, disciplinary action will result.

Administrators may ask, "What sort of disciplinary action can I take?" Just as with an employee, a volunteer catechist can be put on probation, and/or suspended for a time period. Catechists who receive stipends can be given notice of non-renewal.

6. Give the catechist a copy of the conference document stating the first five points and ask the person to comment on the document to ensure understanding.

> This procedure allows the catechist the opportunity to ask for, and be given, clarification of any points.

7. Have the catechist sign the document and add any comments he or she wishes to include; if he or she refuses to sign, have another person witness that fact.

> This other person should be another administrator or the pastor. If neither is available, a secretary or another employee could serve as a witness. Asking a peer of the catechist, such as a fellow catechist, should be avoided.

Avoiding Problems

Although there is no foolproof formula for avoiding documentation problems, careful, objective recording of facts provides the best possible protection. Objective documentation lessens the possibility of misinterpretation and/or multiple interpretations. If an administrator writes, "Mrs. Jones has an attitude problem," one can ask, "What does that mean? An attitude about what? Students? Authority? The Church?" But if one writes, "Mrs. Jones refused to sign up for any of the catechist training sessions, failed to come to necessary catechist meetings, and told students rules governing playground behavior were "stupid," the meaning is clear. Specific documentation enables the administrator to work with the catechist in identifying strategies to improve behavior. Careful, accurate record keeping also protects an administrator against defamation allegations, should the records ever be shared with a third party. It is hard to deny that one said playground rules are stupid, if there were witnesses to that fact; it is easy to deny that one has an "attitude problem" or a "problem with authority."

Practical Considerations

Some administrators ask if every problematic catechist behavior should be formally documented in a catechist's file. The answer is, "Not necessarily." For example, if an administrator notices that a catechist is ten minutes late for class but has never before been late, the administrator may decide not to confront the catechist. However, an administrator might jot a note in his or her calendar or log book noting the tardiness. Whether the information would become part of a written report would depend on whether subsequent problems occurred.

Problems and resentment can often be avoided if administrators ask themselves: Is this the fair thing to do? Is it moral? Is this the action I would want or expect someone to take if I were in the catechist's position? Is it the position Jesus would take? Sometimes it is difficult to balance legal and Gospel issues, but such is the challenge facing catechetical administrators today.

CHAPTER 5

Administrative Liability and the Need for Insurance

As virtually everyone knows, we live in litigious times. It is possible for anyone, even with the best of intentions, to be sued for actions taken or not taken. The catechetical leader is not immune to the threat of lawsuits. Catechetical leaders need to understand the concept of administrative liability and to consider protecting themselves by purchasing professional liability insurance.

Torts

Civil lawsuits brought against administrators of educational programs are generally in the form of tort suits. A tort is a civil or a private wrong. Thus, a person accused of a tort is generally not going to face a prison sentence (unless criminal charges are also filed), but may face fines, loss of property, revocation of certification, and similar penalties.

Tort suits generally can be classified according to four categories in educational settings:

- negligence
- corporal punishment
- search and seizure
- defamation.

Negligence, which is the most often litigated type of tort case, is the topic of Part 1, Chapter 2 in this volume. Every catechetical leader though, should be familiar with the four elements which must be present for a finding of legal negligence: *duty, violation of duty, proximate cause, and injury.* If any one of the elements is missing, no negligence, and hence, no tort can be found to exist. The very meaning of the word *negligence* suggests a lack of intent. Two concepts that should be kept in mind in consideration of negligence are the reasonable nature of the behavior and the presence of foreseeability. All educators are expected to act the way a reasonable person in the educator's position would act. It is the task of the jury or other fact-finder to determine whether a person's action was reasonable. Educators are expected to take appropriate action to prevent foreseeable dangers. Thus, catechetical leaders would be well-advised to assess potentially problematic areas and events within the religious education program.

Most negligence cases occur in classrooms because that is where most students spend their time. However, there are other areas that are potentially more dangerous than the classroom and, hence, a greater standard of care will be expected. Examples would be outside activities, such as play or athletics, and field trips. (See also Part 2, Chapter 4: Athletics and Other Types of Physical Activities)

Another potential area of negligence is that of *child abuse reporting*. While states differ in their requirements of *who* must report, administrators can be held liable for injury occurring to students if they knew or should have known that the child was in danger and failed to report the situation to authorities. The best defense for a catechetical leader in a negligence case is the development of reasonable policies and rules for the safety of young people. The reasonable catechetical leader is one who supervises catechists in their implementation of rules. (See also Part 1, Chapter 4: Child Abuse Laws and the Catechist)

Corporal punishment is a second type of tort. While it may appear that corporal punishment has no place in a religious education setting, some confusion may result from an inaccurate understanding of what constitutes corporal punishment. Any physical contact that could be construed as punitive can be considered corporal punishment. If a child is injured as a result of physical contact with a supervising adult, charges of assault and battery may result and the administrator may be sued under the doctrine of *respondeat superior,* let the superior answer. (See also Part 1, Chapter 4: Child Abuse Laws and the Catechist)

A third type of liability is presented by the tort of *search and seizure*, also discussed in a separate chapter. While the United States Supreme Court has ruled that public schools will be bound by a reasonable, rather than a probable cause, standard, no such restriction exists in private educational settings. Nonetheless, catechetical leaders should have some kind of policy for searching students and/or seizing their possessions. Searching a student should require more cause than searching a locker. Catechetical leaders could be subject to tort suits if harm is alleged to have been done to a student because of an unreasonable search. Thus, the wise catechetical leader will have search and seizure policies in place and will ensure that all staff are familiar with them. (See also Part 2, Chapter 2: Search and Seizure and Other Issues of Privacy)

The last tort, *defamation*, is also the subject of a separate chapter. It is important to note, however, that defamation is the violation of a person's right to reputation, and can encompass both what is said (*slander*) and what is written (*libel*). The potential for defamation certainly exists in adult relationships with young persons.

It is important that catechetical leaders and catechetical staff be factual in their comments, whether oral or written, about student performance and/or behavior. (See Part 2, Chapter 6: Defamation of Character and Catechetical Programs)

The Need for Insurance

No matter how careful and competent a catechetical leader is, he or she may one day face a lawsuit either for administrative actions or for the actions of one under the supervision of the catechetical leader. It is highly recommended that catechetical leaders, like all other professionals, have liability insurance.

The National Association of Parish Coordinators and Directors of Religious Education (NPCD), through the National Catholic Educational Association (NCEA), offers the opportunity for catechetical leaders and other full-time educational employees to obtain liability insurance at a very reasonable cost. This plan is entitled *Professional Liability Protection Plan for Educators* and is available to members of the NPCD/NCEA. It offers protection in the following scenarios:

- injuries to students
- improper placement of students
- improper instructional methods or failure to educate (educational malpractice)
- hiring or assigning unqualified persons
- violation of civil rights
- negligent supervision.

A million dollars of coverage is available for a nominal fee. A catechetical leader may assume that the parish or diocese has coverage. However, the coverage may be minimal and/or may exclude certain situations. The coverage may also be cumulative, which means that the limit of coverage must include all cases filed for the year. In this day of suits routinely asking for $1,000,000 in damages, a $1,000,000 limit on all suits in a parish or diocese for a year may not go very far. Thus, it is advisable for all Catholic educational administrators to carry liability insurance.

While the coverage described above is not available for part-time employees or for volunteers, volunteers are often covered under their home owners' policies. The wise catechetical leader will investigate liability coverage and will present options to all who work in the ministry of religious education.

Pastors and diocesan administrators often give consideration to underwriting the cost of liability insurance for administrators as part of a benefit package.

Catechetical leaders are not exempt from lawsuits. Protection from liability is available and should be thoroughly investigated. For information about NPCD/NCEA professional liability protection call the Forest T. Jones and Company, Inc. administrator at 1-800-265-9366.

Part 4:

Orienting Catechists to Legal Issues: A Guide

This final section of your handbook offers recommendations for in-service sessions on legal issues for use with catechists, aides, substitutes, board members and others involved in your program(s). A variety of in-service ideas are given in order that you can choose the most appropriate approach for your situation and for the persons working with you in the ministry of religious education.

The suggestions offered will make reference to the companion volume created for catechists, *Religious Education and the Law: A Catechist Handbook* (printed under separate cover). You will note that Parts 1, 2 and 3 of that companion volume, parallel the first three parts of this volume, created for catechetical leaders. The *Catechist Handbook* is designed to be given to catechists, substitutes, aides, board members, etc., for their reference during the year. You may wish to provide each with their own copy to keep. Or, you may find it preferable to offer the handbooks to catechists and others for their use during the year, asking that they be returned at the end of the term. To order the *Catechist Handbook* use the order form at the end of this book.

In this section of your handbook Chapter 1 gives general, basic recommendations for conducting in-service sessions on legal issues as well as some optional approaches to addressing various legal issues. Chapters 2, 3 and 4 give further, more specific suggestions for each of the topics treated in the *Catechist Handbook*. These specific suggestions include a "true-false pretest", covering all the topics addressed in that part of the *Catechist Handbook*, and also a list of discussion questions on each of the legal issues addressed.

CHAPTER 1

Conducting In-service Sessions on Legal Issues

Planning for an Effective In-service

By planning ahead and being prepared for your in-service, you will ensure a profitable meeting. The following are some basic planning tips.

Several Weeks in Advance

Determine what you hope to accomplish in the meeting and plan the program with those goals in mind:

- read the relevant section in this handbook and the corresponding summaries presented in the *Catechist Handbook*
- determine the most appropriate format for discussion
- decide who should attend
- invite participants, provide details (e.g. schedule, agenda,

etc.) and distribute *Catechist Handbooks* if prior preparation for the session is called for

- anticipate questions and prepare responses
- reproduce the pre-test so that each person will have a copy
- have any other supporting materials duplicated and organized into packets.

Preparing to lead the discussion

No matter how you decide to present the content to your participants, the most important step is to read the relevant chapters in this volume and the corresponding catechist summaries in advance of the session — more than once, if necessary. This will help you to anticipate the types of questions persons may ask and will assist you in developing an outline of important topics that should be discussed, clarified or explained.

On the day of the session

Make sure the room is set up properly (conference style, e.g. rectangular, oval or round conference table or tables set in a hollow square or hollow rectangle configuration, is best for discussion) and any equipment is in place; make sure other needed items are in place (e.g. note pads and pens/pencils, flip chart, markers and easel, chalkboard, chalk and erasers); make sue that supporting materials/handouts are in place; check on facilities (parking, restrooms, etc.) and refreshments.

At the start of the session

Welcome participants; introduce participants or have them introduce themselves; review the agenda and/or objectives of the meeting; describe the format of the session and explain what role the participants will have; open the session with a prayer.

During the session

State the topic at the beginning of each segment; encourage participation by directing the discussion in a low-key way, by involving each member singly and together, by asking open-ended questions and by reinforcing comments; steer the discussion; restate relevant points; correct any misunderstandings as soon as they arise; don't let one person dominate the discussion.

At the conclusion of the session

Summarize the discussion (a flip chart or chalkboard will be especially useful at this point); review any goals or challenges; make any other announcements; thank participants.

Various Approaches

The following ideas offer approaches that can be used to address the issues to be treated in an in-service session. They offer options for addressing all the issues together or treating issues individually. These suggestions can be adapted to fit your purposes. They can be used in sessions with catechists, substitutes, aides or board members.

- Ask participants to share their greatest legal concerns as an opening exercise. These concerns could be listed on newsprint, chalkboard, or flip chart and used for discussion after the summaries have been read. Identify which situations can be addressed based on the the concepts in the written material available in these resources. Explain that other issues need to be deferred until you can gather appropriate information/resources from you diocesan catechetical office and/or diocesan legal counsel.

- Ask participants to read an individual summary and have them discuss the material and its application to your program. Encourage members to share related educational/ legal dilemmas they have experienced. Would any of the concepts in the written material have been helpful in dealing with these situations?

- First, have participants read the entire set of summaries for a given section (eg. Part 1: Legal Issues the Professionalism of Catechists) and follow with a short, general discussion session. Then, focus on each individual summary.

- Ask participants to read a single summary and come prepared for discussion of the topic.

- Ask participants to read the catechist and family handbooks before a session, or similarly, to review relevant parish/diocesan policies and or handbooks prior to a session.

CHAPTER 2

In-service Resources For Part 1: Legal Issues and the Professionalism of the Catechist

True-False Pretest

Have participants take the following five question, true-false pretest as a "warm-up" activity covering all the topics addressed in Part 1.

1. The U.S. Constitution governs religious education programs.
2. Since parish religious education programs are charitable in nature, there is no liability for injuries resulting from negligence.
3. Persons who copy copyrighted materials for educational purposes

do not have to worry about copyright violations.

4. If a catechist is sued for child abuse, the catechetical leader, pastor, and diocese can be sued as well.

5. Sexual harassment is unwelcome conduct of a sexual nature.

6. Children suffering from AIDS may be denied religious education services.

(Answers: #s 1, 2, 3 and 6 are false and 4 and 5 are true, as indicated in this volume and in the catechist summaries.)

Discussion Questions

Ask if participants need clarification of any terms. Participants may ask the following types of questions, or you may want to encourage discussion and reflection by using these questions or developing others of your own related to your program.

Topic 1: Religious Education and the US Constitution

1. Since the Constitution does not apply to our programs, how can we ensure fairness?

2. Reviewing our parish/diocesan policies and procedures do they all treat people with the dignity that is due them?

3. What behaviors should be expected of catechists, staff members and volunteers? How do we best address parents and students who speak of their constitutional rights in our setting?

Topic 2: Negligence and the Catechist

1. What areas of our facility pose special dangers? What needs to be done to ensure safety?

2. How can catechists make known concerns about safety issues?

3. What documentation would be helpful to all?

Topic 3: To Copy Or Not To Copy

1. Are there special areas of legal concern with regard to copyright law?

2. How can we best ensure that all catechists understand and take responsibility for copyright law?

3. What areas of our religious education programs are "copyright lawsuits waiting to happen?"

Topic 4: Child Abuse Laws

1. Does everyone with responsibility for children in our religious education program understand the child abuse reporting laws for our state? our diocese?

2. How do we ensure that all catechists comply with state law?

3. What is the policy and procedure for reporting child abuse and how do we appropriately address parental concerns in this area?

Topic 5: Sexual Harassment

1. Can each of us define sexual harassment?

2. Give an example of an incident of sexual harassment that you witnessed or heard reported.

3. Do we need to better educate catechists and students about the importance of treating each individual with dignity?

Topic 6: AIDS, Blood-borne Pathogens and Other Diseases

1. What are our parish/diocesan policies regarding AIDS and other blood-borne pathogens?

2. Do our catechists and other staff members understand and practice universal precautions?

3. In what ways can we better strive to be accepting of all students who come to us, even if they suffer from illness?

CHAPTER 3

In-service Resources for Part 2: Legal Issues and the Responsibilities of the Catechists

True-False Pretest

Have participants take the following five question, true-false pretest as a "warm-up" activity covering all the topics addressed in Part 2.

1. There is very little legally that a religious education program can do to enforce behavioral standards.
2. Students in religious education programs have no legal privacy protections.

3. So long as what is said about a student is true, a catechist or other staff member cannot be sued for what he or she says.

4. Off-site service programs and other activities do not to be as closely supervised as on site programs.

5. Athletic programs are no more dangerous than regular instructional programs.

6. Since catechists are not licensed by the state, they are not expected to keep student communications confidential.

7. The appearance of inappropriate involvement with young persons can present legal problems for catechists and other staff members.

(Answers: #s 1-6 are false and 7 is true, as the chapters and summaries indicate.)

Discussion Questions

Ask if participants need clarification of any terms. Participants may ask the following types of questions, or you may want to encourage discussion and reflection by using these questions or developing others of your own related to your program.

Topic 1: Student Rights and Catechist Responsibilities

1. What behavioral expectations do we have for our students?
2. How do we enforce these expectations?
3. How can we best ensure that the rights of all are protected?

Topic 2: Search and Seizure and Other Issues of Privacy

1. What are our parish/diocesan policies and guidelines regarding search and seizure?
2. How do we want catechists and staff members to handle situations in which a search of student persons and/or belongings seems necessary?

3. How do we guard the legitimate privacy expectations of students?

Topic 3: Community Service Programs and Other Off-site Activities

1. If we have a service program, do we have appropriate safeguards in place?
2. If we do not have a service program, do we want to consider one?
3. Do we have adequate personnel and volunteers to supervise off-site activities?

Topic 4: Athletics and Other Types of Physical Activities

1. What kinds of athletic or other physical activities are our students involved in as part of our religious education program?
2. Do we have competent individuals supervising these activities?
3. Are there additional safeguards we should consider?

Topic 5: Keeping Confidences of Young People

1. Do all catechists understand the rules concerning keeping and revealing student confidences?
2. Are any of our catechists requiring students to keep journals? Do they read these? Have they set ground rules for the experiences?
3. Are persons assisting with retreats and facilitating sharing opportunities adequately prepared? Do they know what to do if students reveal that they have been abused or that they are planning to hurt themselves or others?

Topic 6: Defamation of Character and the Catechist

1. Do all catechists understand what is meant by defamation of character?
2. What kinds of situations call for special caution in guarding reputations?

3. How can we be sure our written communications are both truthful and respectful of reputations?

Topic 7: Catechist/Student Relationships

1. Have our catechists been given some in-service training regarding appropriate staff/student relationships?
2. What would be some indications that boundaries have been crossed?
3. How can we develop policies that will clearly state expectations in this area?
4. How do we deal with parent concerns that a catechist or other staff member is "too close" to his or her child?

CHAPTER 4

In-service Resources for Part 3: Catechists and Legal Issues In the Administration of Catechetical Programs

True-False Pretest

Have participants take the following brief true-false pretest as a "warm-up" activity covering the two topics addressed in Part 3 of the Catechist Handbook. Note that three of the issues addressed in the *Catechetical Leader Handbook* are not included here in that they are issues pertaining to the role of the catechetical leader.

1. The Catholic Church, as a charitable institution, is protected from liability in most lawsuits.

2. Catechist and family handbooks can be viewed as contracts.

(Answers: # 1 is false and # 2 is true, as the relevant chapters and summaries indicate.)

Discussion Questions

Ask if participants need clarification of any terms. Participants may ask the following types of questions, or you may want to encourage discussion and reflection by using these questions or developing others of your own related to your program.

Topic 1: Handbooks for Catechists and Families

1. Are our handbooks adequate? If not, how can we go about developing and/or revising them?
2. What areas identified above need attention in our handbooks?
3. Are parents required to sign statements that they have read and agree to be governed by the handbook?
4. Do we need a committee to identify issues for handbook inclusion?

Topic 2: Boards of Religious Education

Questions for use with board members

1. Does our board have all the legal information it needs?
2. What are special areas of legal concern for board members?
3. How can we best develop policy?
4. What areas of our religious education programs are "lawsuits waiting to happen?"

Questions for use with catechists

1. Do we have recommendations for the board regarding policies needed? policies in need of revision?
2. What legal concerns would we like to make known to the board?

Order Form

Qty	Amount	
____	$_____	*Religious Education and the Law: A Handbook for Parish Catechetical Leaders;* $12 member/$16 non-member
____	$_____	*Religious Education and the Law: A Catechist Handbook**

(Each pack includes 10 handbooks)

Qty	Amount	
____	$_____	1-4 packs $20 each pack member/ $26.00 nonmember
____	$_____	5-8 packs $19 each pack member/ $25.00 nonmember
____	$_____	9 or more $18 each pack member/ $24.00 nonmember
____	$_____	single copy $5 member/ $6.60 nonmember

*The Catechist Handbook is designed to be given to catechists, substitutes, aides, board members, etc., for their reference during the year. It addresses the same legal issues in summary form, highlighting the catechist's role and responsibilities.

Additional Resources:

Qty	Amount	
____	$_____	*Making Commissions Work: A Handbook for Parish Religious Education Boards/Commissions.* 1996. 104pp. $15 member/$20 nonmember
____	$_____	*A Primer on Law for DREs and Youth Ministers* by Sr. Mary Angela Shaughnessy. 64pp. 1992. $5 member/ $6.60 nonmember
____	$_____	*Pathways of Faith: The Story of Today's DREs* - Video Cassette. 1994. 14 minutes. $14.95 member/ $19.95 nonmember
____	$_____	Total

Please send your order to: or Tele: 202-337-6232
NCEA Publication Sales   FAX: 202-333-6706
1077 30th St., NW, Suite 100
Washington, DC 20008-3852

❑ Payment enclosed. (No charge for shipping and handling.)
❑ Bill me. Minimum order $25. Shipping charges will be added.

Name _____

Parish/School _____

Address _____

City_____State_____Zip_____

Tele:(_____)_____